"Wild Bill" Hickman and the Mormon Frontier

"Wild Bill" Hickman and the Mormon Frontier

HOPE A. HILTON

SIGNATURE BOOKS, SALT LAKE CITY

1988

*To all of Bill's descendants,
including my own five*

Copyright © 1988, Signature Books, Inc., Salt Lake City, Utah.
Signature Books is a registered trademark of Signature Books, Inc.
Printed in the United States of America.
All rights reserved.

Book and cover design by Connie Disney.

Hand tinted cover photo by Jeanie Hanks and Heather Tuttle.

LIBRARY OF CONGRESS CATALOGING-IN-PUBLICATION DATA

Hilton, Hope A.
    "Wild Bill' Hickman and the Mormon frontier / Hope A. Hilton.
       p.   cm.
    Bibliography: p.
    Includes index.
    ISBN 0-941214-67-2 (pbk.)
    1. Hickman, William Adams, 1815-1883. 2. Mormons—Utah-
-Biography. 3. Utah—History. 4. Peace officers—Utah—Biography.
5. Frontier and pioneer life—Utah.   I. Title.
F826.H64 1988
979.2'02'0924—dc19
  [B]   88-18600
                                                                                                                 CIP

Contents

Preface	ix
1. *The Call of Mormonism*	1
2. *To Follow the Prophet*	9
3. *The Rocky Road to Zion*	17
4. *Zion at Last*	27
5. *The Green River Ferries and Fort Bridger*	35
6. *Return to Green River*	43
7. *Fort Bridger and Margaret*	51
8. *Brigham's Mailman*	59
9. *The Utah War*	67
10. *The Dust Settles*	83
11. *The "Hickman Hounds" and the Shootout*	87

12. *The Beating of Governor Dawson*	95
13. *The Morrisite Affair*	103
14. *Government Guide*	109
15. *The RLDS in Utah*	115
16. *The Murder of "Spanish Frank"*	123
17. *Wyoming, Death in Peace*	129
Epilogue	135
Appendix	137
Bibliography	143
Index	152

"Let it go, things will be made right someday."

—WILLIAM ADAMS HICKMAN

Preface

A "Mormon mountain man" is in many ways a contradiction in terms. Free-spirited explorers like Jim Bridger, William H. Ashley, Jedediah Smith, and others were often unchurched, single, buckskin-clad pioneers. Although William Adams Hickman (1815-83) was a trusted member of the Church of Jesus Christ of Latter-day Saints (Mormon), husband to ten plural wives, including an Indian squaw, father to thirty-five children, and one of Utah territory's earliest lawmen, he was also an independent, rough, undisciplined mountain man and outlaw. As much at home in his trading post near Fort Bridger as in his more comfortable house in the Salt Lake Valley, and responsible for more deaths than lives saved, Hickman led an enigmatic, eventful life.

There was never a time during Bill Hickman's western experience that stories—often exaggerated—of his usually "notorious" exploits were not related in homes throughout the Salt Lake Valley and elsewhere. His sixty-eight years took him from Mormonism's beginnings to its periods of isolation and adjustment during the 1850s and 1870s. He died in 1883 a non-Mormon because of an excommunication he considered unwarranted. Hickman's loyalty to the Mormon church and its leaders continued until 1863, thirteen years after his arrival in the Great Salt Lake Valley, when he accepted employment with the United States government. Earlier, he had served his church as one of the most valuable, effective Mormon guerillas harassing federal troops during the 1857-58 Utah War. But after he took a position as a federal Indian guide, Mormon church leaders viewed him as a renegade church "spy," no longer worthy of their support and friendship.

During the past thirty-five years searching for my great-grandfather, William Hickman, I have encountered an extraordinary, complex man. Vengeful, stubborn, and something of a bully, he could also be compassionate, even tender. In 1871 Hickman penned his unforgettably sensational autobiography, *Brigham's Destroying Angel*. Written in haste and anger, it details his killing of about fifty Indians and five whites. The publication of his autobiography and his testimony before a grand jury in September 1871 led to the arrest of Brigham Young and other Mormons whom he accused of master-minding his confessed crimes. In *"Wild Bill" Hickman and the Mormon Frontier* I do not question whether Hickman actually wrote *Brigham's Destroying Angel*. It is too accurate in its details to have been written by anyone else. Instead, I try to determine how much of the autobiography was true and how much of it fabrication.

History has willingly accorded Hickman credit for his misdeeds and personal failings while overlooking many of his contributions to the Mormon frontier. I believe he deserves a more prominent place in Utah and Wyoming history. In attempting to write a more complete biography, I have profited from access to unpublished family sources, relevant archival and photographic materials at the Church of Jesus Christ of Latter-day Saints in Salt Lake City, the Utah State Historical Society, Utah State Archives, the *Deseret News*, the Harold B. Lee Library at Brigham Young University in Provo, Utah, the Library of Congress, the National Archives, the Beinecke Library at Yale University, the Huntington Library in San Marino, California, the Bancroft Library at the University of California, Berkeley, court records of Lee County, Iowa, and state historical records in Sweetwater and Fremont counties, Wyoming. At Signature Books, Gary J. Bergera, Brent Corcoran, Connie Disney, Jani Fleet, Ron Priddis, and Susan Staker helped steer the manuscript through various editorial and production stages. In addition, I have appreciated and benefited from the support and encouragement of Leonard J. Arrington, Davis Bitton, Golda Busk, Tom Hickman, Leona Holt, Minnie Woodring, and especially Ron Bitton and my husband, Lynn.

I have relied on Hickman's *Brigham's Destroying Angel: Being the Life, Confession, and Startling Disclosures of the Notorious Bill Hickman, The Danite Chief of Utah* for facts of

Hickman's life that can be corroborated from other sources. Hickman's avowedly anti-Mormon editor, J. H. Beadle, wrote the preface to the autobiography and the first chapter. He also wrote the bitter diatribe against Young and the Mormons on pages 137-139, probably the first paragraph on page 192, and several other brief inserts, sometimes adding only a single word. Except for these additions, Hickman's mind and hand are the book's undisputed source. Beadle did not have access to Brigham Young's daily office journal or to other sources available today which confirm many of the book's first-hand statements. I have not used footnotes, which can be distracting, but have instead tried to provide enough information within the text to allow the reader to locate the appropriate reference in the bibliography.

To my mind, one of the most compelling questions about Hickman is why he implicated Brigham Young, Hosea Stout, William Kimball, and others both in his book and in court. One of the burdens this biography has accepted is examining the historical events and psychological disposition of Hickman which inclined him toward the apparent betrayal of those whom he had previously so loyally obeyed, without intruding too heavily into the flow of events with unnecessary commentary.

In August 1950, while I was living in Chicago, a friend discovered my tie to Hickman and presented me with a copy of *Brigham's Destroying Angel*. My search for the truth of Bill Hickman began. Twenty-eight years later I discovered in the Utah State Archives the October 1870 murder warrant for Hickman's arrest and the Tooele County probate record of September 1870, which led to the murder. These two previously unknown documents revealed the reasons for the misguided course Hickman took in the summer and fall of 1871 before the grand jury. But the high point of my research occurred in July 1981 when my husband and I, with Mrs. Minnie Woodring of Lander, Wyoming, discovered Hickman's final resting place. Numerous searches over the past fifty years had failed to shed light on Hickman's last days. Mrs. Woodring led us to a knowledgeable old pioneer. Early Sweetwater County land and tax records and newspaper accounts further established the circumstances under which Hickman lived, died, and was buried in the Wyoming wilderness near Lander in August 1883.

My mother always seemed ashamed of her ties to Hickman and never mentioned him by his full name while I was growing up in California. Finally at age twenty-one, after reading official Mormon church historian Joseph Fielding Smith's *Essentials of Church History*, I asked the crucial question: Was the "self-confessed murderer" mentioned in this book my ancestor? My mother, not one to accept criticism even of a dead ancestor she seemed ashamed of, defensively justified Hickman by saying, "He killed a Mexican who stole his wife. Brigham Young told him to do it, and he was excommunicated from the church." (Actually, as I later learned, Hickman's excommunication occurred more than two years before the shooting of Frank Moreno, but family traditions die hard.)

"Wild Bill" Hickman's grave in the mountains west of Lander, Wyoming, was kept a secret from all but his first wife, Bernetta, and three of his grown children and their spouses. Other Hickman descendants were never told. Evidently, the end of their progenitor's life did not match his promising beginnings. Hickman's life has never been recounted before except by Bill Hickman himself, and even then the story was incomplete. I hope this book succeeds in approaching a clear, insightful portrayal where Bill himself, for whatever reason, was unwilling or unable to tell the truth.

– 1 –

The Call of Mormonism

William Adams Hickman was a frontiersman from birth to death. Born on 16 April 1815 in a log cabin in western Kentucky, one of America's first frontiers, he was given the first name of his paternal grandfather, as was customary for a first son, and the maiden name of his mother for an identifying middle name. Sixty-eight years later, on 21 August 1883, in a sod-covered dugout, a few family members hovering nearby, he died in central Wyoming, one of the country's last frontiers. The telegraphed news of his death, sent by his two sons-in-law from Lander, Wyoming, to Salt Lake City's *Deseret News*, was reported in the metropolitan cities of the East by people who could only dream of western frontiers.

For the last twenty-four years of his life Bill Hickman carried a bullet lodged in his thigh, leaving him a partial cripple with a "shuffling gait," unable to haul freight, ride a horse without pain, or earn sufficient money to care for his large polygamous family. During these last years he suffered greatly. Mercifully, the pain ended with his death in 1883. Poverty, coupled with disgrace, stalked him to the end. Far from Utah's populated centers Hickman found solace in the wilds of central Wyoming, a confirmed addict of the alcohol and drugs he took to alleviate his pain and perhaps to bolster his wounded ego. He died fifteen years after the railroad tied America together by ribbons of steel, altering America in ways he could scarcely comprehend. He remained faithful to the horse and the sturdy buckboard wagon. At the time of his death, and without his consent or encouragement, landmarks had been named after him in two states, including a hill, a fort, a canyon, a creek, a knoll, three springs, two gulches, and a basin.

Bill Hickman's ancestors settled in Kentucky in 1810. Previously, they had been neighbors in Culpeper County, Virginia, and in Surry and Stokes counties in North Carolina with the Isbell family. The two families had intermarried for three generations, producing in most cases a Protestant mix of sturdy stock, light-skinned, blue-eyed descendants, often distinguished by their quick and awful tempers.

Bill was an eighth generation American. His first American ancestors were Nathaniel and Avis Hickman who came from England to Northcumberland County, Virginia, before 1653. More than a century later, during the American Revolution, his great-grandfather Edwin Hickman, with his wife Phoebe and several close Isbell relatives, moved from tidewater Virginia to North Carolina in the hopes of improving their economic situation. None of Bill's direct ancestors fought in the Revolutionary War, but according to Bill, "twenty-one of his relatives did."

The Hickmans and Isbells were impoverished burned-out-land tobacco farmers in Virginia at the time of the Revolutionary War. Needing new land to survive, they chose Surry County, North Carolina (later divided into Stokes and Surry counties), on the border between North Carolina and Virginia. This area contained vast unsettled tracts of heavily wooded land, green to saturation. It was bisected by narrow streams, including the Dan River, the largest and longest, and by mountain gullies. It remains much today as it was then, with tobacco growing and drying the main concerns of the "hill-country" populace. Schools did not exist when the Hickmans farmed there and are still lacking today in a few isolated communities.

In 1810, led by Bill's grandfather William and his eighteen-year-old son, Edwin Temple, Bill's future father, the family moved again. The revolution was over and cheap, fertile land called pioneers through the Cumberland Gap into the newly opened state of Kentucky. The family chose Warren County, near the western border, where Bowling Green, the county seat, was still a cluster of log cabins. The move was made in early summer or late spring as soon as the roads were dry, so unfortunately neither the

North Carolina census taker nor the Kentucky census rolls of June 1810 include the Hickmans and Isbells, who were still in transit. Fortunately, yearly tax records, recording every male Kentuckean over eighteen years of age, confirmed their arrival. From 1811 to 1819 it is known where Bill's parents were living, whether they owned slaves, and how much land they farmed.

Edwin Hickman, Bill's father, found a wife in 1813 when he was twenty-one: Elizabeth Adams, a new arrival in Warren County from Culpeper County, Virginia, where Hickman ancestors had lived some twenty-five years before. Elizabeth, according to family tradition, was "a redhead," perhaps accounting for the dark auburn, or reddish, hair of her first child, William Adams, born in 1815. Elizabeth had a distinct advantage over her husband: she had not spent her childhood in the backwoods of North Carolina and had been educated. Edwin's eighteen years in isolated Stokes County, North Carolina, left him an illiterate farmer throughout his long life. He died in Missouri in 1888 at the age of ninety-six, outliving his oldest son Bill by five years. Like the Hickmans and Isbells, all immigrants were seeking cheap land or trying to claim their war land grants.

The area the Hickmans chose to settle was about ten miles south of Bowling Green. (Today it is Alvaton, hardly less rural now than then, with a population under five hundred.) Bill was only three years old when the Hickmans acquired legal title on 27 February 1818 to the one-hundred-acre plot on the Barren River on which they had probably been squatters. County records disclose that they paid $1.00 for the land which belonged to the heirs and widow of William Work. If the Hickmans had been squatters, the Widow Work must have died or abandoned the property. Kentucky had a large influx of so-called "squatters" at the time, people who settled on farm land that seemed unclaimed, and state courts were favorably inclined toward encouraging the development of unworked land.

Before young Bill's fifth birthday, the alluring cry of more and better land called his parents and grandparents out of western Kentucky to Missouri, to the north and west. In 1819, eastern families traveled to Missouri by flat-boat along the Missouri River, America's first dependable highway system. This time the Isbell relations stayed behind in Warren County, perhaps afraid to venture one more time into the unknown to seek their fortune. The journey was not an easy undertaking. Bill was barely four years old, a younger brother, James Barton, was three, and a new baby sister, Lettice, was not more than two months old in July 1819 when they set out. Grandparents also made the journey, as well as Bill's only Hickman aunt, Rhoda, a five-year-old sister of his twenty-seven-year-old father.

William and Lettice Hickman remained close throughout their lives to their only son, Edwin. Theirs was an extended family born of necessity. They always lived in the same house, farmed the same land, and no doubt Bill's "Aunt Rhoda" was more like a sister than an aunt as he grew to manhood.

Neither Bill's mother Elizabeth nor his baby sister Lettice would have been strong enough to attempt a rigorous river trip before the coming summer, the best time for traveling anyway. Spring flooding would be over and the weather would be warm. Their destination was the town of Franklin in the west-central part of the new Missouri territory. The rolling river country of Missouri was no less green and lush than western Kentucky, only more rough and sparsely settled. Missouri was still two years from statehood. Land speculators met each flat-boat with offerings that encouraged settlers to sink their savings on the promise of a quick fortune. The roads out of Franklin were muddy with undrained swamps, but the immigrants were experienced and faced them with courage.

Grandfather William was forty-nine years old and knew this would be his last move. He had lived in three states and chased his share of rainbows. He had been willing to gamble one more time. After a few weeks the Hickmans bought a piece of land in Chariton County, later Randolph County, where they settled for the next thirty years.

Young Bill matured rapidly in the wild countryside where he claimed in his memoirs to have killed wild boars, wild cats, and bears before his sixteenth birthday.

Edwin was elected magistrate of Randolph County, an office he held for six years from 1822-28. He also built and operated the first grist mill in Randolph County. Bill writes that his father was "a quiet man, not given to fighting or drinking." Bill slopped the hogs owned by his father and grandfather and did farming chores, preparing to be an ordinary Missouri farmer. But life held more in store for Bill. Perhaps, if he could have seen what lay ahead, he would have been content to remain a Missouri farmer fighting only droughts and stubborn mules.

Bill's impulsive behavior showed at an early age. In later life it would prove to be his downfall. At the age of fifteen he was sent away to school by his parents to study medicine, but he gave it up shortly and turned to the study of law. This also proved boring. A third attempt to acquire an education resulted in his being sent to Huntsville, the Randolph County seat six miles to the east, to room and board with the family of George Burckhardt, the county's legislative representative, who had hired a scholar to teach his own children. Bill's delayed decision on education was interrupted again when he fell in love with Burckhardt's daughter, Bernetta. Although three years his senior, Bernetta reciprocated his affection. She was captivated by the impulsive, dashing Bill, who could ride a horse better than most men. It was Bill's first experience with love, and nothing could dissuade him from an early marriage to beautiful black-eyed Bernetta. His parent's admonitions to finish his education first fell on deaf ears.

Bill had come to Huntsville from a smoke-filled log cabin. The Burckhardts, on the other hand, lived in a two-story frame house built on Huntsville's main street. To the rough, barely educated farm boy, the Burckhardts must have appeared awesome, representing political clout, money, and position, things Bill hardly knew.

Despite their age difference nineteen-year-old Bernetta fell in love with sixteen-year-old Bill, undissuaded by his abrasive surface. Apparently she saw qualities in Bill that earned her life-long loyalty over fifty years. In spite of hardships and poverty, not to mention Mormon polygamy, obstacles that might have lessened the ardor of a less dedicated woman, Bernetta remained by Bill until his death. She dismissed the sheltered life she might have had as unimportant.

Both the Hickman and Burckhardt families disapproved of the budding romance; the Hickmans because of their desire to see their oldest son get an education, and the Burckhardts because Bill seemed below their social standing, and his age and lack of education were less than impressive. Although later Bill wrote, "our parents consented" to the marriage, a Burckhardt relative still living in Missouri in 1965 gave a different account of the circumstances surrounding Bill's and Bernetta's marriage.

According to Burckhardt family history, a midnight elopement was planned by the teenage lovers. They wisely waited until

Bill's seventeenth birthday in April 1832. To implement their escape a string was tied to Bernetta's big toe. The string hung out from her upstairs bedroom window to where Bill could reach it on horseback. Bernetta could not sleep; the anticipated pull on her toe had driven sleep from her mind. Finally Bill came. He helped Bernetta to climb down to his horse and together they rode all night to another town where they were married the next day by a justice of the peace.

Anxious parents awaited their return. Fortunately, the new couple was welcomed back after their marriage. Next, Bill tried teaching school, but his seventy-five unruly students convinced him to earn a living in another way. Bill's father gave him a nearby tract of prairie and timber land in October 1832 and told him to go to work. He built a house, fenced his farm, and by the time he left for Illinois to join the Mormons in 1838, he had 320 acres with good buildings. In the summer of 1832, while he was still teaching school, there was an Indian outbreak north of Huntsville, the eastern overflow of the year-long "Black Hawk War" in Illinois. Bill wanted to join the fray, but school trustees declined to let him go. He was disappointed—not realizing that his future would include many days of Indian fighting. A popular war in which more than 7,700 men volunteered for two weeks to six months at a time, it only ended with the battle of "Bad Axe" where the Sac Indians under their great chief Black Hawk were either killed or driven west of the Mississippi. Several years later savvy politicians would use their enlistments in the Black Hawk War to garner votes. One young soldier, A. S. Johnston, resigned after the victory in 1834 but later rejoined to fight Indians and Mormons on the frontier. Bill would become one of Johnston's most dangerous adversaries.

Bill's Missouri farm was located on the north side of the Illinois-Missouri road; well-traveled, it was the main east-west crossing bisecting Missouri. The eastern boundary of his farm was the dividing line between Randolph and Macon counties. The Mormons from Ohio began traveling along this road on their way to Jackson County, Missouri, in 1831, where they intended to build their New Jerusalem. At the time Bernetta was a member of the Methodist church, and early in 1833 Bill also converted. Bill's conversion helped the young eighteen-year-old assume a more respectable place in local society. Bill's parents were not churchgoers or members of an organized religion. Not until 1867, when he was past seventy-five, did Bill's father finally join the Methodist church. Bill's exposure to Mormon fervor in 1833 no doubt led him to investigate the new religion and, according to his autobiography, "to make theology his principal study for two years."

By 1834 the tide of Mormon immigration brought more than a few travelers past Bill and Bernetta's farmhouse. The settlers were tired and hungry as they began the final one hundred miles of their long journey to their new zion. Bill writes that he "almost daily" held conversations with the ragged army of Mormons and often sold or gave them food because he felt sorry for them. The hostility with which many Mormons were greeted by local farmers was common knowledge. The Mormons needed water for themselves and their animals, and Bill's well soon became a regular stopping place. In an interview years later in Utah, Alvin Nicols of Brigham City recalled Bill's friendliness: "I first saw [Bill Hickman] in Missouri. He went to his field, got some corn, ground it in a coffee mill and made the finest bread I ever ate."

Hickman was inexplicably drawn to these strange people and their gospel. Their clothes were often in rags, their boots worn and caked with mud. Greenlief Burckhardt, Bernetta's brother, became caught up in the fury and gossip about the Mormons and was horrified to hear that his brother-in-law Bill was accused of being friendly to them. He made a trip by horseback from Huntsville five miles away to question his sister and her husband about the current gossip. Much to his consternation he discovered that Bill was feeding hungry Mormons at his own table and asking Bernetta to cook for them. The news upset him. He became enraged and challenged Bill to a fist-fight. This proved unwise, as Bill "whipped him good."

Missouri governor Lillburn W. Boggs's "extermination order" against the Mormons—that the Mormons be forced to leave the state or be exterminated—in October 1838 convinced the Hickmans they could no longer delay joining the persecuted sect. Their baptism probably took place in the Middle Fork of the Salt River adjacent to their farm. This river flowed sluggishly eastward to the Mississippi, their next destination. According to a letter written in 1872, Hickman never regretted his baptism. But neither parents nor in-laws ever understood this decision to abandon the farm and to follow instead the Mormon prophet and his strange teachings.

By this time, Bill's physical appearance had matured and his reputation as a ruffian was growing. He would later be described by three contemporaries writing in the 1860s: an Iowa settler, the English explorer Sir Richard Burton, and anti-Mormon writer J. H. Beadle, all of whom agreed on certain aspects. To the Iowan Bill was "tall, raw-boned, sandy-haired and of a florid complexion, strong and sinewy, in height about six feet, though appearing taller." Cold-grey piercing eyes proclaimed him "a villain... who hesitated at nothing." Burton's description was of "a good-looking fellow, about forty-five, rather stout and square, with a high forehead, open countenance and mild light-blue eyes." Beadle, who knew him best, says that "he was a man of heavy build, round head, and somewhat awkward, shuffling gait; five feet nine inches in height, and with bright, but cold-blue eyes, hair and beard dark auburn — the latter now tinged with gray — and a square solid chin. His vitality is evidently great, and his muscles well-developed."

Blessed with a strong athletic body, well developed from the farm and gristmill, Bill would later acquire burned and leathered skin from riding the open range. His strength allowed him to endure injuries that would have killed a less toughened man. His menacing blue-grey eyes—eyes that would never need glasses—would develop a permanent squint from long days of riding in the summer sun and cold blasts of winter.

Everything else being equal, by the late 1830s Bill could outshoot most men with the pearl-handled Colt or Yaeger revolvers, hung from a heavy black leather belt, slung around his hips.

– 2 –

To Follow the Prophet

In the spring of 1839, Bill Hickman sold his 320-acre farm for "a low figure" to his brother Josiah and to Richard W. Shipp and left for the gathering place of the Mormons. He placed his wife and four children in a buckboard wagon filled with less than adequate supplies and headed east along the same Missouri-Illinois road which had first brought the Mormons into their lives. They headed toward the Nauvoo area where they would live for one year before "moving out into the country" in Adams County, Illinois.

Typical spring and summer weather greeted the travelers. Rain fell almost nightly; often they were drenched during the day as well. The children, ranging in age from six-year-old Elizabeth to two-year-old Edwin Thomas, fought off exposure and sickness. Only Elizabeth and four-year-old Sarah Katherine would survive the ordeal. Bernetta was pregnant again. The expected child, named Rebecca, and Joshua, born in 1842, would also become early victims of the hardships the Mormons would face in Illinois.

Hickman and his young family arrived in Nauvoo in late April 1839. On 6 May, Hickman met Joseph Smith, Jr., who ordered Bill ordained to the Council of Seventy the same day. On 12 May, the Council of Seventy delivered to William Adams Hickman a letter of recommendation. A hunter since his youth and handy with a gun, Hickman seemed a natural choice to be one of the bodyguards of the prophet Joseph. A similar call was extended to Hosea Stout, Orrin Porter Rockwell, and Lot Smith, all of whom had grown up on the frontier. Dressed in white, surrounding their beloved prophet, these four men would have made an impressive sight.

After being introduced in Nauvoo, Bill decided to settle in Lee County, Iowa, directly across the Mississippi River from Nauvoo. He purchased land adjacent to the river in Nashville, (later named Galland), six miles below Fort Madison, the county seat.

One hundred Mormon families had already settled in and around Nashville. The previous "Old Settlers" grew anxious over this apparent foreign invasion. The Mormons bought part of the town of Keokuk, all of Nashville six miles north, part of Montrose, plus several thousand acres of the "Half-Breed Tract" in Lee County—land originally set aside by the U.S. government for the descendants of fur traders and their Indian squaws but since appropriated by white land speculators.

The threat of growing Mormon political power led to the formation of an anti-Mormon political faction whose main goal was to force the Latter-day Saints from Iowa territory. In this embattled atmosphere, the Mormons were accused of many crimes, including murder, robbery, and larceny. As one "Old Settler" wrote, "Our citizens can scarcely any longer exercise a peaceful forbearance. Every old settler has lost something. No one feels secure."

A list was compiled of seventeen "known thieves" and their crimes. The accuracy of these charges will probably never be completely known. All of the accused, including Hickman, "escaped from justice and forfeited their recognizances and securities running away to Nauvoo." This seems to be the first in a series of legal encounters that would follow Hickman throughout his entire life. On 8 October 1841, he was indicted for stealing 300 pounds of bacon, worth about $40, from John Wright "on or about the first day of May, 1841." (John and Ferguson Wright were leaders of an anti-Mormon coalition to oust the newcomer Mormons from Lee County.) Ordered to appear before Judge Charles Mason in the "United States vs. William A. Hickman" were defendant Hickman and five witnesses for the prosecution: Emory Jones, John Gillilam, Samuel and John Henderson, and Ferguson Wright. According to the History of Lee County, Hickman was "sent to jail in Lee County, but never tried." Bill, however, says he was never in jail. Court records confirm that no trial was held in October 1841.

In fact, Bill appeared before court clerk O. H. Rich on 11 October 1841 to ask that his trial be delayed until he could obtain the deposition of three witnesses who, he asserted, "can clearly establish the facts." As the trial date approached, and county sheriff William H. Walker served subpoenas on the witnesses, Hickman took refuge in Adams County near Quincy, Illinois, south of Nauvoo.

It seems improbable that Hickman and his young family could have eaten the 300 pounds of bacon, and that the theft, if it occurred, was actually Bill's attempt to harrass the Saints non-Mormon persecutors.

The next year, Hickman was having trouble in Adams County. On 29 October 1843, Leonard H. Crow signed an affidavit of complaint against Hickman, saying he "feared bodily injury because of threats leveled against him by said Hickman." The following 30 January justice of the peace J. P. McCann issued a warrant for Hickman's arrest. Hickman appeared with Daniel Leanderback. They pleaded guilty and were released upon promise of good behavior, which was backed by a $200 bond and all their land and chattel, according to district court records.

That March Hickman was arrested again. The Saints were being burned out of their homes, and their animals stolen. Hickman struck back and was arrested for destroying and stealing property. He appeared with Wilkins G. Salsbury and Presley T. Matthews to answer the charges before Peter Lott and Timothy Kell, justices of the peace in Adams County. The three men acknowledged they owed the State of Illinois the sum of $250, to be levied against their goods, chattels, lands, and tenements. Hickman was ordered to appear the first day of the court's next term in Quincy, Illinois, to answer a charge of larceny.

On 5 June 1844, word reached Nauvoo that Joseph Smith had been arrested in Quincy. Early the following morning Hosea Stout, Tarleton Lewis, Bill Hickman, and four others started in a skiff from the Nauvoo landing for Quincy to rescue their prophet. A heavy headwind delayed them, and they arrived at their destination in the evening, after Smith had already left for Nauvoo in the company of two officers.

Three weeks later, on 27 June, Smith and his older brother Hyrum were murdered at Carthage Jail, Illinois. Hickman was in Huntsville, Missouri, with Bernetta, who was awaiting the birth of their seventh child at her parents' home in Huntsville. As soon as the news of the prophet's death reached Huntsville, Bill returned to Nauvoo, anxious to be of assistance. He found that Joseph's death had thrown the Saints into turmoil. But in a few days Brigham Young's forceful personality had rallied many of the Saints to his leadership and that of the apostles. Hickman was quick to volunteer his services and promised loyalty to the new prophet.

However, throughout 1845 schisms arose in the church, as men with some authority demanded more. One who caused considerable dissension was Joseph Smith's hot-tempered younger brother William, who was also an apostle. Action was taken in a closed session of the Council of Twelve Apostles, advising William to leave the city. Brigham Young asked Hickman to help engineer William's escape from Nauvoo and the anti-Mormon mobs who had killed his brothers. No doubt, Young also wanted to be rid of William's potential threat to his own new authority. Hickman rode with William until they reached the border of northern Iowa.

That Young succeeded in leading the main body of the church to Utah can partly be attributed to the men he chose to assist him. Young assigned Hickman to oversee covert spying activities, to "subdue" the enemies of the church, and to serve as his chief bodyguard. Hickman and others in a tightly knit group served Smith in Nauvoo and Young in Winter Quarters (Florence, Nebraska), Council Bluffs (Kanesville, Iowa), and crossing the Great Plains. Then, in the Great Salt Lake Valley, the same group acted as the first lawmen, serving Young whenever trouble erupted, whether with Indians, outlaws, or Gentiles. From 1850 to 1853, they shared the duties of government with Young's secret political organization, the Council of Fifty. Their skills contributed to the survival of the entire body of Mormons, and Gentiles picturesquely labeled Young's strong-arm lawmen "Destroying Angels" and "Blood Avengers." In 1860 British explorer Richard Burton, writing of this group, called them "desperados." He identified a triumverite of Ephraim Hanks, Orrin Porter Rockwell, and Bill Hickman, whom he termed "the leader of the 'Danites.'"

The term "Danite" referred to a quasi-official band of zealous Mormons who during the late 1830s in Missouri tried to revenge Mormon wrongs. It was later misappropriated by non-Mormons during the Nauvoo and territorial periods of Mormon history to describe the Nauvoo Legion, territorial militia, and hired guns. Hickman was not a Mormon during the Danite heyday in Missouri, and there is no reliable evidence that the Danites, as such, survived after 1838 as an organization. However, that some vigilante Mormons, notably Hickman, continued to espouse the Danite philosophy they had been taught by church leaders of "attacking the Gentiles to preserve the Saints" seems apparent. To the end of his life, Hickman believed that in every instance of violence directed toward non-Mormons he had done the right thing not to submit to persecution but to fight back.

In the winter of 1844 Hickman paid a visit to a Colonel Williams, supposedly the man who commanded the black-faced mob which shot and killed Joseph and Hyrum Smith. Hickman was trying to bridge the gap between Mormons and non-Mormons, an assignment that was repeated in the years to come. According to Hickman, Young sent him on the mission primarily to learn if Williams and others intended to rise against the Mormons again. Young reportedly was satisfied with the information Hickman brought back, and this solidified a friendship and trust between the two men which endured until problems erupted many years later.

Pressures on the Saints in Nauvoo continued to build in the wake of the Smith murders. Antagonists wanted the Mormons to leave the state and enumerated the crimes of the Mormon people. The practice of polygamy was largely secret, but rumors persisted. Minerva Wade, who later became Bill's third wife, wrote of the period:

> To teach polygamy openly in Nauvoo was forbidden-yet at the same time it was public knowledge among the Saints. I know polygamy was preached by Joseph Smith. I heard Ira Hatch say the Prophet had a revelation that would cost him his life when it was made known. The Prophet said, "It must come forth no matter what it costs me." There was so much hatred already that it was not preached public for fear of mob violence but Joseph Smith had wives sealed to him besides Emma: Eliza R. Snow, Destimony Fullmer, Lucy Walker were all well-known to me. Lucy Smith Walker said the Prophet said if she would live with him as a wife she would have a son that would be a great man—but he did not urge her knowing the persecution that would follow. After the martyrdom of Joseph Smith, these girls were all working at the Nauvoo Mansion, a big hotel. Lucy Walker was waiting on table. After the martyrdom Heber C. Kimball, one of the

Twelve Apostles, was sent to tell the girls who had been sealed to Joseph Smith, not to leave but to choose among the Twelve Apostles and remain with the Church. He told her she had a right to make her choice. He had been so kind and sympathetic that she decided he would be a good husband [and] there and then promised to marry him which she did. She regretted she had not complied with Joseph Smith's request—he had been killed and she had no offspring from him—so she made up her mind such a thing should not happen again and she had a child by Heber C. Kimball in polygamy at Nauvoo. The babe was kept in hiding. My mother nursed it—Lucy had to appear in society. The baby died at Winter Quarters when near a year old. Parley P. Pratt took other wives before Joseph Smith died named Malinda Wood and Huldah Frost. The girls used to go and see the immigrants come on the river on the boats. After unloading the boats passed Nauvoo going further up the river with cargo.

The Nauvoo Charter, which incorporated the Mormon city, was revoked by the Illinois State Legislature on 29 January 1845, seven months after the martyrdom. An understanding was reached with Hancock County officials that the Mormons would leave the area in the summer of 1846. Every available building in Nauvoo was converted into a shop where wagons, harnesses, and other items necessary for the journey west could be made. On 2 February, church leaders decided to leave before the ice on the Mississippi had broken and before church leaders could be arrested on counterfeiting charges from undelivered but promised indictments issued by federal marshals in St. Louis. If the threat of arrest was a ruse it worked. There was a last rush to participate in the ceremonies in the Nauvoo temple, where Bill and Bernetta received their "endowments" on 30 January, at which time Bill was also married to a second wife, Sarah Luce. Almost nothing is known of Sarah beyond what appears in Brigham's Destroying Angel, although her three brothers later played a prominent role in Bill's life as members of his "gang."

As a part of these Nauvoo temple endowment rituals Hickman promised to avenge the blood of Joseph Smith. Mormon apostle Heber C. Kimball recorded in his diary on 21 December 1845 that "I have covenanted, and never will rest nor my posterity after me until those men who killed Joseph & Hyrum have been wiped out of the earth." As Hickman himself later explained to his daughter Katharine, "After the assassination of that great and good man Joseph Smith the Prophet of God, I took a solem Oath to stand up against all opposition that might come against the Latter-day Saints and specially for those who might stand at the head of Gods Kingdom." In many ways, Hickman's future activities would reflect his understanding of what he believed to be a sacred oath.

According to Hickman, Sarah Luce traveled to the Salt Lake Valley in 1848 with her father, who is not identified by name. Sarah may have become romantically involved with one of the other pioneers because when Hickman arrived in the valley in 1849 he found a newborn son a few days old. He says he never had children by Sarah yet later writes boastfully, "I had children by them all." (This is one of the contradictions in Brigham's Destroying Angel.) Sarah apparently never lived with Bill in the valley, although her son was raised under the name Hickman to cover her "indiscretion."

Polygamous families were the first to leave Nauvoo so as to protect the church from further disclosures of the controversial practice. Families trying to salvage property crossed and re-crossed the river several times. Hickman left with Sarah in the first crossing and later returned for Bernetta.

The organizational talents of Brigham Young kept the exodus from becoming a disaster. Hickman's military bent was apparent, and in addition to serving as bodyguard, he was appointed captain in the artillery company of Colonel John Stott. Hickman's primary assignment was to spy on the church's enemies in Nauvoo (such as Colonel Williams), although he was also occasionally given orders to execute punishments. Bill Hickman rarely shirked an assignment from Young, but like most he expected some compensation besides praise for a job well done. When the tenuous balance between duty and reward tipped, when his family suffered for lack of money and food, Hickman's seething anger erupted.

– 3 –

The Rocky Road to Zion

Minerva Wade, Bill Hickman's third wife, was fifteen years old when her father Moses drove their wagon onto a river barge headed toward the Iowa shore. Years later in Utah she wrote: "We left Nauvoo in April, 1846—crossed the Mississippi. The boys sang, 'Get Out There for California—We'll Make Our Way to California,' to the tune of 'Old Dan Tucker.'"

Hickman was already on the trail by the time Minerva left in April. For Hickman the march across Iowa was a "hard and lasting journey"; he was already impatient with the slow travel required for the four heavy pieces of artillery and some 500 stands of small arms. He arrived at Council Bluffs, Iowa, in time for the recruitment call by non-Mormons Thomas L. Kane and Captain Allen of the First U.S. Dragoons to fight in the Mexican War. Hickman had contracted measles on the trail and was too sick to volunteer for the Mormon Battalion. He was probably also too sick to participate in the farewell ball given under a great arbor of poles and branches the night before the battalion's departure.

When he was well enough to travel, Hickman returned to Nauvoo to help his family make the trip to Iowa. But he also had an assignment from Brigham Young to assist the poor who were having difficulty starting on the trail. He arrived in Nauvoo by late August or early September 1846 in time to join the men searching for Phineas Young and Brigham H. Young, both of whom had been taken prisoner. According to Hickman, they searched for ten days before finding the two men unhurt. Almost immediately thereafter a mob started shooting cannons toward Nauvoo, marking the beginning of the Mormon war that took place in early September.

On the second day of battle, Hickman and several other men fashioned two homemade cannons—made from a steamboat's shaft and fixed upon wagon wheels with cannon balls hammered out of pig lead. The mob had three cannons. According to Hickman, the Mormons' homemade cannon shot kept their enemies at bay. Hickman never learned how many were killed. A report that sixteen men were loaded into a wagon suggests the extent of the damage inflicted on the mob. Hickman and others mention that Captain Anderson and another cannoneer were killed on the Mormon side. This Nauvoo war lasted several days. Hickman confessed that he "had been anxious from a boy to be in a battle" but added, "This fight took a great deal of starch out of me. My appetite for such fun has never been so craving since."

In the end the Mormons surrendered mainly because their forces had dwindled to fewer than 100 men, and on 16 September they agreed to accelerate their departure from Nauvoo. Hickman claims the mob requested a dozen Mormon prisoners—including himself. According to his autobiography, he tried to escape in disguise but was apprehended at the river's bank. He was seized, arrested, and taken to prison, where he was shackled with six feet of logging chain attached to a fifteen-pound iron ball.

William Clayton makes no mention of prisoners being taken, although Daniel Wells says Phineas and Brigham H. Young were kept as hostages. There is no record that these two were mistreated. According to Hickman, after a few days he knocked down his jailor, presumably with the fifteen-pound ball, and took his bowie knife and pistols. Despite rumors, no evidence indicates he killed the jailor. This was the only time, Hickman later wrote, that he was kept in jail.

According to the history of Lee County, Iowa, written in 1879, "Bill Hickman and his band would steal before one's eyes in the light of day. If a Mormon coveted the corn or the horse of an honest farmer, he went and took it . . . Thief and murderer was Bill Hickman. It is said that before he became notorious as a murderer, he stole a large number of horses from farmers and others in different parts of the country. He was caught with one of the stolen animals in his possession and arrested." The only indictment ever issued against Hickman in Lee County of which there is any record was for stealing bacon. Perhaps the other crimes Bill is here accused of were borrowed from *Brigham's Destroying Angel* and incorporated as part of the county's history.

The remaining Saints hastily abandoned Nauvoo and trudged across Iowa. They established a camp and log town, known as Cutler's Park, on the Nebraska side of the Missouri River. Indian problems caused their relocation three miles north at Winter's Quarters and on the east of the Missouri River at Council Bluffs, Iowa, which soon mushroomed into a boomtown of 16,000 before the Mormons left in 1852. Mormon apostle Orson Hyde was a prominent figure in the new communities. Brigham Young had appointed him caretaker for all the Saints along the upper Missouri. Hyde's influence was felt beyond the bounds of Kanesville because of the newspaper he also edited, *The Frontier Guardian*. He was involved in politics and saw to it that all elected officials of Pottowattomie County were Mormons and Whigs.

Bill Hickman spent a year in southern Iowa before joining the Saints at Florence, Nebraska, or "Winter Quarters," in the fall of 1847. He raised a crop but also found that considerable profits could be made gambling. According to local residents of Lee County, he owned a fast black stallion and would bet on his horse, encouraging others to bet against him. It was fun and easy money. Brigham Young recognized the problems gambling could create among the Saints and not only warned Bill against his gaming instincts but asked for Bill's race horse as a gift for his ten-year-old son Brigham, Jr. Bill reluctantly surrendered his horse, fearing that if he refused Young would cast a curse upon him.

Most surviving evidence reveals that Bill Hickman, Brigham Young, and Orson Hyde were close friends. Perhaps the events recounted in Hickman's autobiography account for these bonds. According to his memoirs, Hickman killed a half-breed Indian who had joined the Mormon church but subsequently threatened Young's life. Later, he killed a notorious horse-thief who was seeking revenge against Hyde. Hickman admits to both killings and claims they were the first acts of violence performed at Young's request. Young gratefully promised to make him "a great man in the Kingdom" some day. As Orson Hyde rose in prominence, he became a target of dissidents. The *Frontier Guardian,* which he started about this time, attacked in print a gang of eight to ten counterfeiters. Hickman waited one night in the dark for the counterfeiters and then destroyed a portion of their press, effectively putting them out of business. According to Hickman, Hyde "said I had again saved his life." Hyde would later go to great lengths to defend Hickman, who blamed Young for their later disagreements.

In the spring of 1848, Brigham Young left Nebraska for his second and last journey to the Great Salt Lake Valley. Before leaving he requested that Bill stay behind to protect Hyde, who had been appointed leader of the 1849 immigration, the largest and one of the poorest groups to make the trip to the Great Basin. Hickman wanted to go with Young but obediently stayed, saying goodbye to Amasa Lyman, Young, and his new wife, Sarah Luce, who was traveling with her father in the wagon train. Hickman rode thirty miles with the train to the Elkhorn River, hoping Young would change his mind. He did not.

During late 1848 and early 1849, Hickman traveled back and forth along the now familiar Iowa road, repairing wagons and aiding families stalled on the trail. Bill also helped to build houses for the Saints in Council Bluffs.

Mail service was a major problem for every frontier community. Mail contracts, awarded by the federal government, were eagerly sought by those who could provide men and horses. In 1848 the hundreds of Mormons gathered at Winter Quarters wanted a dependable mail service badly enough for church leaders to petition Washington, D.C., directly, requesting that "without delay a semi-weekly mail service be started to the Pottowattomie Indian purchase lands in the State of Iowa." Signatories included Brigham Young, Heber C. Kimball, William A. Hickman, and, beneath his name, "George W. Hickman," in slightly disguised handwriting. George W. Hickman was living in Mississippi, so William Hickman signed his name for him.

The petition proved effective, and in the spring of 1849 Bill received at least two letters from his brother and father living in Missouri. The postage marks on both read "Pottowattomie County." (His father and brother wanted to know about "gold-hunting" at the Great Salt Lake.) Bill received the first letter prior to his departure in early May 1849; the second must have been carried to the Salt Lake Valley by one of the region's earliest mail carriers, Ephraim Hanks or Almon W. Babbitt.

Also preparing for the 1849 Mormon migration were Sally Maria Bundy Wade, her husband, Moses Wade, and their three adult daughters, including Minerva Wade who would become Hickman's third wife. In 1833 near Farmersville, New York, son Edward had been the first Wade family member to join the Mormon church. By 1839 all had joined. Sally Maria had to be lifted from a sick bed into the waters of baptism, walking the next day for the first time in more than seven years.

Moses and Edward Wade joined the Mormon Battalion in 1846, leaving Sally Maria, who was still ill, and three daughters to fend for themselves. The Wade women, stranded at Council Bluffs for nearly two years, endured prairie fires, near-drownings, and scurvy. Sixteen-year-old Minerva wrote about their trials:

> Prarie Fire December 1st. 1846. Two hundred miles above Canesville a company wintered—Dunkin Johnson was away up in Montrose by Swift River. I traveled from Mt. Pisgah in company with Martha Lewis. I was sixteen and she was fourteen. We lived with my sick mother, whose health was poor since we were forced from our burned home near Nauvoo by the mob, and Mrs. Dame an invalid. Steps had been cut down to the river to get water. Mother prayed, "Oh Lord preserve my dear child and give her strength to carry water to help put out this terrible fire."
>
> Mrs. Dame wrapped up the bread in one bundle and the baby in another and if worst came to worst, I the strongest, was to take one bundle under each arm and rush through the fire. Mrs. Dame was in very poor health and never revived after the fire. She died.
>
> My mother Sally Maria Bundy Wade was never able to do anything after. I had to chop wood for two years. Mr. Dame had gone to Missouri to work and earn something to live on and go on—to the west the next spring. He had left men to do the chores but they soon left and I had to do everything. I got scurvy, flesh rotted off the ends of my ankles. I could not wear shoes but had rags tied around my feet and wandered out in the snow to cut and carry wood.
>
> A prarie fire was set by Indians. One spark was seen, in a few minutes the whole country was in flames. Bank fires were set. Water [was] carried and fire put out. Only damage, one wagon burned—one load of hay. Everything else pulled to the bank of the river for safety.

At "Mosquito Creek," east of "Miller's Hollow" (near Council Bluffs), Minerva wrote:

> A temporary bridge had been laid by pinning cottonwood logs together. The ends were tied to each other then bored through the two with a large auger just made to fit the holes and then the stringers of the bridge were made. These were covered with brush which [was] also found down the river.
>
> A heavy rain had fallen—Mary had already passed safe over the bridge before—the stream was not large in dry weather—when my company came it had rained to a torrent. The water was running three feet over the bridge. But the company was anxious to go on. So they crossed the bridge in spite of the water. All got safe over but my father Moses Wade's last wagon. The oxen heaved and the wagon which was very heavily loaded with flour went off the bridge.
>
> I and two younger girls were in the back of the covered wagon. Horace Drake rushed to the back of the wagon, pulled out his pocket knife and while the other men held the wagon—cut a slit in the cover and pulled us girls out. Then the wagon went down—many were carried into the stream forever swept under.

As Sally's condition worsened, Minerva promised her dying mother that she would never leave the Mormon church. When Sally died in January 1848, Minerva buried her mother by herself, alone and grieving. Minerva's sisters had returned to New York to the more comfortable life they had known before conversion. Minerva, a redheaded nineteen-year-old with freckles, was no beauty, but in Hickman's mind her youth apparently made up for her plain looks. She needed help to reach the valley. When Bill proposed marriage, she accepted. They were married in Council Bluffs on 1 May 1849. In his autobiography, Bill calls Minerva "a good industrious woman, kindhearted and agreeable." They had eight children, six of whom later married and had large families.

Bernetta, Bill's first wife, had given birth to her eighth and last child the summer before, a daughter also named Bernetta. To distinguish her from her mother, she was called "Kitten." Not only did Kitten survive her birth at Winter Quarters in 1848 but grew up to bear ten children of her own. She would later blame Brigham Young and polygamy for her family's problems. Kitten's niece recalled her saying in 1916 that "if God himself came down and told me polygamy was right, I wouldn't believe him."

In 1848 Orson Hyde discovered that many of the Saints' cattle were disappearing, evidently stolen by a band of Omahas. The Omahas could sneak back across the Missouri River to their protected Indian lands, from which the pioneers were barred by government decree. Hickman took it upon himself to locate the culprits and eliminate them. According to his autobiography, he stalked three Indians into their protected area. There he killed two of them who turned out to be Pawnees, not Omahas. He returned late the next night to bury the dead. In the meantime, before the discovery of the bodies, he helped a government contractor recover 1,000 stolen head of oxen. He claims to have been paid so well that he finally had enough money to purchase a good outfit for the trip to Salt Lake City the following spring.

When the government Indian agents later discovered the two bodies, they demanded that the guilty party be brought to trial. The finger of responsibility pointed to Orson Hyde.

According to the first edition of the *Frontier Guardian*, 7 February 1849, Hyde cleared his name by inducing Bill to swear before a justice of the peace, J. G. Bigler, the following testimony:

> Personally appeared before me, J. G. Bigler, a Justice of the Peace in and for said county, on this fifth day of February in the year of our Lord, one thousand eight hundred and forty-nine, William A. Hickman, who being duly sworn according to law, deposeth and saith: That whereas certain reports have been put into circulation by some evil designed person or persons prejudicial to the character of Mr. Orson Hyde and that also of my own: I do hereby solemnly declare that Mr. Hyde never induced me to commit violence upon the person of any man, either white or red. Neither has he ever tried, by day or night, in public or private to persuade me to injure any person, neither did I ever do anything of the kind at his instance. However much I may differ in matters of the church from Mr. Hyde, I feel that it is a duty that I owe to him, and particularly to myself and family to make the above statements; and further this deponent saith not.
> William A. Hickman

Before Hickman's departure west in the spring of 1849, he became involved in another Indian skirmish, this time on Hyde's orders. He killed an Indian who had first shot two arrows at him. Because this incident followed so soon the murders of two others, Hyde felt compelled to punish Bill publicly by expelling him from the Mormon wagon train to which he had been assigned.

Hickman and his wives left that same evening, going twelve miles along the western trail and joining a "Colonel" Cornwall's wagon train bound for the California gold fields. The Colonel and Bill became fast friends. The Colonel claimed he had fought and killed many Indians, making him a hero in Bill's eyes. Most, he said, had been killed in the "Black Hawk War" of 1832 in Illinois—the war Bill had regretfully missed while still a Missouri school teacher.

The Colonel was probably a confidence artist in search of an appreciative audience, for a search of the names of the more than 7,700 volunteers in the Illinois "Black Hawk War" discloses only one person named Cornwall, a private named Alexander Cornwall.

On 1 June 1849, Hyde wrote a letter to Brigham Young from Kanesville, explaining what had happened and why Hickman and his family had departed before the 1849 migration: "Brother Hickman has gone to the valley. You may hear some bad accounts of him, but don't kill him till I come! It may be that my testimony may have a little bearing in his case! He is sometimes a little rash and may shoot an innocent Indian, mistaking him for an Omaha horse thief!"

Eleven months later, on 25 April 1850, Hyde, still in Winter Quarters, wrote to his brethren in the Great Salt Lake Valley on the same subject:

> Tell William A. Hickman that I have had a talk with the Pawnee chiefs and braves today, and have settled by treaty the difficulty occasioned by his visit to Carterville. I gave them a barrel of flour last year, and paid fifty dollars today, and now *it is all right.* This fifty dollars or the case for which it was paid, has saved many dozen horses for us.
>
> We cut Hickman off, it is true, because of such a wonderful pious attitude against him, but if the people at Carterville had not fed and fostered the Indians, contrary to our counsel, there would have been no Indians killed there.

Hyde's letter suggests that Hickman was disfellowshipped or excommunicated. He was rebaptized into the Mormon church, according to records of the Jordan Ward in 1852, possibly suggesting a measure of repentance for the two Indian deaths.

Reports that Hickman had been seen on the trail were relayed to Orson Hyde, who was anxious to learn if Hickman was still faithful and in Salt Lake City. John D. Lee, a friend and former bodyguard to Joseph Smith, reported that on 3 August 1850 Hickman crossed with the Benjamin Jones family in the Charles Stevens Company at Ford Number Four over the Sweetwater River. On 4 September, Almon W. Babbitt, carrying the mail from Salt Lake City to Kanesville, reported to Hyde that Hickman had been seen beyond the South Pass. Both news reports were printed in the *Frontier Guardian*.

− 4 −

Zion at Last

Bill, Bernetta, Minerva, and Bernetta's four children arrived in the Great Salt Lake Valley on 20 August 1849. They moved into Pioneer Fort where new immigrants were housed until other accommodations could be arranged. According to Hickman, on the day he arrived in the city he attended "a big dance with the Mormon girls" with his new found friend, Colonel Cornwall. Bernetta and Minerva, both pregnant, were probably left at the fort or in the wagon while Hickman and the Colonel danced with the young women.

Pioneer Fort stood on the southwest side of the new city, where Pioneer Park is today. In her memoirs, Minerva described her experience there:

> The first winter was a terrible one with deep snow, in some places the houses were drifted over and fences covered. . . . I was living in Salt Lake City in the Southwest corner of the Olde Fort in a little adobe house with my husband, on February 14 1850, my oldest son was born. When spring opened we moved over the Jordan River and took up land and made a home between Taylorsville and Bishop Gardner's Mill. We were not successful in getting water out of the Jordan River to water the land, the banks were too high to get the water to irrigate with.

The Hickmans' lot, ten miles south of Salt Lake City in Taylorsville, appears on the original land deeds of Salt Lake County as part of plot number twelve, with 764 acres owned jointly by W. A. Hickman, Jeremiah Meacham, and others. One of these was Orson Hyde, who eventually owned 202 3/4 acres. The closest neighbors were John and Samuel Bennion. On 8 June 1852, School District Twenty was organized in Taylorsville, and William Hickman's property marked the southern boundary.

Early on Hickman must have become discouraged with farming. Instead he turned to breeding sheep, cattle, and horses in Rush Valley, several miles west of Taylorsville. The herds provided the means to support his growing family.

The Taylorsville Saints obeyed the counsel of Brigham Young and erected a large fort and meeting hall for their protection, eventually called "Hickman Fort." A sanctuary against Indian raids, homes were built inside high walls of wood and stone. A dug-out built into the nearby hill housed Hickman's immediate family. This was known as "the smaller Hickman Fort." The remains of the larger fort could be seen as late as 1980 when real estate developers destroyed the hand-hewn logs from the fort walls.

Under such conditions, neighboring families became very close. Hickman reportedly rescued members of one Taylorsville family when they became stranded across the Jordan River with nothing to eat. According to his granddaughter Eda Kohlhepp Lisonbee's later reminiscence, Hickman waded across the river with water up to his shoulders and a sack of flour on his head. Mormon-Indian relations remained relatively uneventful until February and March 1850 when a minor uprising occurred in the Provo Canyon area of Utah Valley. Other encounters followed on the west side of Utah Lake and as far south as Spanish Fork. In response to such difficulties, Brigham Young ordered the Indians exterminated.

Hickman wrote a detailed account of the ensuing war, as did George W. Bean and Edward Tullidge. Daniel H. Wells and John Taylor each wrote briefer accounts in 1884 for Hubert H. Bancroft's *History of Utah*. Tullidge, writing in his *History of Salt Lake City*, was not a participant in the war. Hickman portrays himself as a hero who turned defeat into victory after persuading leaders to change their tactics. Significantly, none of the others mention Hickman's heroism.

Still all accounts agree about the major events related to the two- or three-day battle. The trouble started when an Indian was murdered by three Provo settlers. In response the Mormon militia marched south to Provo under George D. Grant. Daniel Wells, commanding general of the militia, arrived the next day. One militiaman and at least eight Utes were killed. Several days of pursuit followed, during which some twenty or more Indians were killed. Wells declared martial law and called all the men of the area into service. The Indians barricaded themselves in Rock Canyon, where the snow was two feet deep.

Evidently, the Indians surrendered after as many as forty braves and five whites were killed and several wounded. Both Tullidge and Hickman mention that twenty or more sick Indian children and their widowed mothers, totalling about one hundred women and children, were left behind and were later taken in by Mormons. The local Mormons were called on to feed and care for the starving Indians and to persuade the Indians to raise grain and to provide for themselves.

Hickman brags about beheading Chief "Big Elk"—because Jim Bridger had offered one hundred dollars for the head—and wrapping the head in a blanket after displaying it to the other men. However, "Big Elk" actually refers to "Old Elk," who died of exposure and measles several weeks later following one of the battles around Provo Lake.

In his "Reminiscences" Wells describes "the battery on truck wheels carrying a cannon," which preceded the Mormon troops. He does not say the battery was designed to scare the Indians from their hiding places. According to Hickman, this was the plan of attack suggested by the militia officers—a plan Hickman thought ridiculous. In his autobiography Hickman wryly wonders whether "it was the want of brains, or too much canteen [i.e., alcohol] that had caused such plans."

Hickman's church calling at this time was to herd stock belonging to the Mormon church. In these years much of the church's net worth was measured in cattle, as men and women often paid their tithing in "kind" rather than in "specie." The largest herd was kept in Rush Valley. According to Hickman, he was not paid for his work. In his account of his visit to Utah in 1860, Richard Burton wrote that "Bill was somewhat notorious for meddling with Church property," implying that Hickman may have rustled some cattle, embezzling what he thought he was owed.

But Hickman was still a respected family man and citizen. On Tuesday, 29 July 1851, a meeting of the men living in the

Western Jordan Precinct convened. Joseph Harker and Samuel Bennion were appointed judges, and William Hickman became clerk of the Western Jordan Precinct.

Hickman decided to take a fourth wife, Sarah Basford, the widowed daughter of his partner in the Taylorsville land holdings, Jeremiah Mecham. Sarah and Bill were married on 18 August 1850, when she was sixteen. They had four children between 1856 and 1864.

But in August 1851 Hickman "got the gold fever" and departed for California, leaving behind his wives and five children, with Minerva eight months pregnant. According to Hickman the wagon train he joined insisted on making him captain, as his reputation as an Indian fighter "was known to them." It was not an easy trip. Indians had scalped immigrants in a wagon train in front of them only two weeks earlier. Hickman's party discovered the remains, which he described in grisly detail.

Later, when the immigrants encountered Indians, Hickman tells of killing and scalping some thirty-two Indians. A "Doc Ripley" in the party, he writes, wanted a fresh Indian scalp and said to Hickman, "Captain, take off the scalp for me, as your hands are bloody." But when Hickman began to cut, the Indian, who had only been superficially wounded, jumped up. He then killed the Indian with his knife. Such stories of Indian fighting could easily be dismissed as exaggeration, but Hickman obviously did something to have earned the reputation as an Indian fighter.

In California Hickman mined for gold at the famous Placerfield diggings where, he says, everyone knew him as "a Mormon" and regarded him with curiosity. The pay was about forty dollars per day, certainly more than he made caring for church livestock. He remembers his first experience with "miner's law," when two thieves were hung, a punishment justified by the voice of the crowd. Hickman proposed whipping instead, he writes, but was ignored. According to Hickman, he made $10,000 in a tunnel-digging operation—which he characteristically soon lost. Ten months later he returned with a party of eight on good horses and pack mules.

During Hickman's absence, a neighbor named Tanner tried to collect a bad debt from one of Hickman's wives. On 25 November 1851, Brigham Young addressed the following letter of reprimand to "Brother Tanner."

> I understand you have taken a yoke of oxen from Sister Wm. Hickman on account of debt against him-obtained through gile by claiming it was for a loan and now you refuse to give them up which leaves Sr. Hickman without means of transportation. If you had a claim against him you should have stopped him from going to California. Therefore it is considered best for you to return the oxen, cow or other property without delay.

Several reports had reached Hickman while in California that Young was having difficulty in Utah territory with the newly appointed federal judges sent from the east. In Hickman's memoirs he writes, "they and Brother Brigham couldn't hitch horses." Other problems were occurring on the Green River. On 12 February 1850 the Mormon legislature had granted "ferry rights" to the Mormons. Mountain men already operating well-established ferries did not appreciate the competition.

Young's office journal for 3 July 1852 records Hickman's return to the valley. That Young hoped to enlist Hickman's help with at least one of the problems he faced was soon clear. Hickman brought home "a few hundred dollars to make his family more comfortable." The precise figure was probably $500, because the following day Young's office journal records that "Bill Hickman came in and paid $50.00" tithing. Then he was summoned to "a long meeting" in Young's office.

The clerk's minutes of the meeting indicate it was also attended by Thomas Bullock, Daniel Wells, Willard Richards, Orson Pratt, Wilford Woodruff, Charles C. Rich, Truman O. Angel, Edward D. Woolley, William W. Phelps, Heber C. Kimball, Edward Hunter, Nathaniel A. Felt, Joseph Young, and George A. Smith. Young led the men in discussing the subjects of drinking, stealing, and persecution. Young commented, "If the Saints had been as holy as the Angel Gabriel, persecution would have been just the same."

About this time the old and feared name of "Danites" was resurrected by the Gentiles and applied this time to a group of "Minute Men, who were often at the beck and call of Brigham Young when trouble erupted." From time to time, Young referred to a certain group of men as "his boys." This group included Bill Hickman, Orrin Porter Rockwell, R. T. Burton, George Boyd, George Grant, and William Kimball.

Friction began to develop in 1852 between Jim Bridger and Louis Vasquez at Fort Bridger and the Mormons in Great Salt Lake City. On 8 June 1852, Bridger and Vasquez appeared in the city and swore out a complaint against "a certain immigrant whose name they did not know." They claimed he had a horse with the familiar "BV"—Bridger/Vasquez—brand on it, "which, if it had been legally bought, would have had the brand reversed by the owner before it left his possession."

Probate court judge Elias Smith issued an order to have the horse returned, as it had been acquired "felloniously." Lewis Robison, whose life and name would later become entangled with Fort Bridger, appeared before the same probate judge on 28 June 1852 and swore out a similar complaint against "a certain immigrant."

As the winter of 1852 approached, Young asked Hickman, by this time one of the president's appointed lawmen, to keep watch on Ike Hatch and his gang. Ike was suspected of stealing horses and cattle and may have been the "certain immigrant" of the past June, who was guilty of rustling from Bridger and Vasquez.

According to Hickman, he watched Hatch for two or three months. He found he was stealing cattle and reportedly selling the butchered meat to Young and his special friends, who were no doubt buying the stolen meat unwittingly.

Ike was cornered and shot by Hickman in "Big Field" south of Twenty-First South in December 1852. Not a clean shot, Hatch lingered painfully until 10 March 1853. Young recorded in his journal the shooting of "The Notorious" Ike Hatch by Hickman on 11 March 1853. Hatch was not the first "notorious" criminal to be dealt with in this way in the fledging city.

Several members of Hatch's gang continued to steal horses. Hickman writes that on 2 April 1853, after conferring with Young, he and several friends, including a "Mr. R.", presumably Orrin Porter Rockwell, took the Old Indian Trail up to Fort Bridger to apprehend the thieves.

At Fort Bridger, someone told Hickman the gang he was seeking had been seen in Echo Canyon. Hickman and an eighteen-year-old companion named Joe set off to find them. They waited until morning, when they could better follow the thieves' tracks in the newly laid snow. Four men were spotted about two miles away shooting at wild geese.

Hickman and Joe had Colt revolvers, and Joe began to tremble at the prospect of trying to capture four angry men. Hickman says he slapped Joe's face, telling him bluntly, "Obey orders and follow me." The four fugitives were captured, and Hickman's other companions soon arrived. They discovered the thieves' camp and three stolen horses belonging to Mr. R. According to Hickman, there was sufficient evidence that one of the four was guilty to send him "down the river with a bullet hole through him."

On reporting to Young, Hickman and Mr. R. were told they could divide the recovered goods between them. Mr. R. later found and killed the last of the gang, a man named Vaughan.

Hickman bitterly remembers this as the high point of his services to Brigham Young: "It is all I ever got for services rendered on Brigham Young's orders. Neither did I ever receive a present from him, not so much as one dollar." When writing his book in 1871, Hickman was destitute. He was surrounded by prosperous pioneer men, many of whom had come to the valley years after he had, men who now lived in fine houses with barns and land.

By 1853, Hickman was almost constantly in the saddle, riding through the territory hunting wanted men. There were so many criminals, mostly emigrants on their way to California, that the Salt Lake City Council voted to construct a penitentiary. A ten-acre plot in "Big Field" (Sugarhouse) was selected, and by the end of 1854, the territory's first prison was completed. By January 1855 nine occupants were behind adobe prison walls, twelve feet high and four feet thick. Prior to this, convicts could occasionally be seen cleaning Main Street with balls and chains shackled to their ankles.

By October 1853, the local LDS bishops' census showed 18,206 Mormons in the territory. Of these, 5,979 lived in Great Salt Lake City, and 2,273 in Salt Lake County. This same year, Hickman would be asked to center his life in the Green River region of the territory, miles away from its populous center.

–5–
The Green River Ferries and Fort Bridger

In 1853, after a relatively quiet year in the Salt Lake Valley, local Indian tribes began attacking settlements near present-day Ogden in what would become known as the "Walker War," after Chief Wakara. Brigham Young counseled Mormon settlements to build forts for protection. On 15 October, the Deseret News printed the advice from Young given at the recent Mormon church General Conference:

> "Fort Up"—against the Indians. Build a Fort that the Devil could not get into unless you are disposed to let him in. Build Forts first in every settlement. You may refuse to follow this advice and be killed or have cattle stolen. Homes are to be in forts so the Indians can't creep up on you before you are aware . . . that you can be good for a few Indians if they should chance to come upon you. . . . Let every woman and child that can handle a butcher knife be good for one Indian, and you will be safe. . . .
>
> "Chief Walker"—Let him alone. My policy is to give them gifts. Instead of being Walker's enemy I have sent him a pile of tobacco to smoke.
>
> Many appear very bold, and desire to go and bring me Walker's head, but they want all the people in Utah to go with them. . . . I say just give me 25, 50, or 100 men, and I will go and fetch you Walker's head. I do not want his head, but wish him to do all the Devil wants him to do . . . this will chastise people good.

At the same meeting, Mormon apostle George A. Smith also talked at length of Chief Walker and his offenses against the Mormons.

The Saints in West Jordan and Taylorsville, where Hickman lived, had already followed Young's advice. On 8 March 1853, John Bennion wrote in his diary: "commenced to build my house in the Fort."

Meanwhile, Hickman had been convinced by his sojourn in California that money was not to be had in digging gold but rather in selling goods and services to emigrants. Brigham Young agreed. Young's appetite for control of the Green River ferries and Fort Bridger had been whetted at year's end, when the accounting funds were tallied. By December 1852, $1,859.62 had been collected from the ferries; in addition enterprising merchants going to the area from Salt Lake City were required to pay license fees.

The following April, Young asked Hickman to go to the Green River and establish yet another ferry, this time under church ownership. Hickman returned to the Green but found too much competition and too much uneasiness already between the Mormon ferrymen and mountain men. He was afraid of being shot, and to avoid conflict he traveled sixty miles east along the trail to Pacific Springs near South Pass and set up his own trading post on 1 May 1853. This was one of the few times he failed to fulfill an assignment from Young. Young received a letter on 30 July 1853 from D. C. Merrill, who reported that he had been to Hickman's trading post on 2 July, where he "received good treatment and many favors." Also, Merrill continued, Hickman "hosted Captain P. E. Marshall's missionary camp and good feelings prevailed."

Much to Hickman's surprise, his younger brother, George Washington Hickman, stopped at Hickman's trading post during the summer of 1853. Hickman did not recognize him because he had not seen George since 1841. George was on his way to California with a newly acquired medical diploma. Hickman persuaded George to spend the winter in the valley, and "before the winter was over, 'Mormonized' him."

From his 1871 perspective, Hickman commented: "poor fellow, he has never had but one wife, won't practice medicine, lives on his farm, . . . and goes along as though he was a steroyped

Christian indeed." This was hardly true. Hickman failed to mention that his brothers George and Thomas Jefferson both became members of his gang of rustlers. Hickman's code of loyalty and secrecy prevented disclosure of his friends' involvement. George subsequently settled in Salem, Utah, as a farmer-physician, and Thomas became the sheriff of Bent County, Colorado.

The summer of 1853 proved to be an excellent trading season. The trail was crowded with emigrants traveling to Oregon and California and Mormons flocking to Utah. Hickman's location gave him an advantage over Fort Bridger, sixty miles further west. He set up a blacksmithing shop for wagon repair, had plenty of groceries and whiskey to trade, and exchanged lame stock, "two lean for one fat." He even persuaded a Gentile named Doc Morton to set up shop 200 yards from his establishment.

As early as 1848, Brigham Young had written to Jim Bridger requesting that he keep Indians in the Green River area under control. However, Indian troubles around the fort continued. Several months later, Young received a letter from Bridger and Vasquez, warning that Indian chiefs Old Elk and Wakara were planning to attack the Mormon settlements. A letter dated 29 April 1853 from J. H. Holeman, territorial Indian agent, supported Bridger's and Vazquez's warning: "I think it probable we shall have something of a difficulty with a band of the Utah tribe of Indians, under command of the celebrated Chief Walker."

Holeman suspected that Mexican traders, who had been arrested for buying Indian children, were inciting the Indians, but Mormons too were encroaching on Indian lands. Holeman addressed the problem of the Mormon settlements at the Green River several times in correspondence with L. Lea, United States Commissioner of Indian Affairs in Washington, D.C. In November 1852, he wrote:

> I visited immediately—the section of the country—found a company of Mormons under the charter Legislature of Utah, had assembled on Green River, and commenced construction of a bridge; finding much opposition on the part of the Indians, they determined to abandon for the present, and all returned to Salt Lake City—should the Mormons persist in determination, a war will be the consequence.

On 5 March 1853, four months later, Holeman wrote to Lea from the Weber Station in Utah: "The letter last November outlining difficulties between Mormons and the Indians... I fear a disturbance if the country should be settled and occupied by the Mormons, or if they attempt to build bridges and establish ferries, under the acts of the Territorial Legislature." Holeman complained that there had been no mail from the states since October because of snow.

In the middle of the dispute were the claims of the mountain men who otherwise controlled the emigrant traffic across the Green River. A clash of life styles and allegiances guaranteed that peace could never be established until either the Mormons or the mountain men capitulated. Bridger hoped and expected that the Mormons would return to their homes in the east. Young thought only of driving Bridger and his friends out of the area or of neutralizing their influence by preventing the Mormon immigrants from spending their few dollars on Gentile goods.

Bridger was born in 1804. He was forty-nine in 1853, seasoned and trail-wise. As a young man of eighteen years, he had moved to the Rocky Mountain frontier, then in the Mexican territory. He had been a guide to John C. Freemont, discoverer of the Great Salt Lake. Bridger claimed that in 1843 the governor of Chihauhau, Mexico, gave him "possession rights" to 5,000 acres in Green River County on Black's Creek of the Sweetwater River. He was never able to prove he had such a claim, saying he "lost the papers." In 1842 he began building Fort Bridger with his partner, Louis Vasquez. By 1847 when the Mormon migration began, the fort was a well-established stopping place, where supplies could be purchased or wagons refurbished. While proprietor of the fort, Bridger married three Indian squaws in succession and fathered several children. Bridger made the fort his headquarters and home for eleven years until August 1853, when the Mormon militia forced him out.

The Mormon church claimed that the fort was sold in 1853 to Lewis Robison, quartermaster of the Utah militia and Brigham Young's agent. There is no record of payment being made, unless Robison paid from his own funds, which is doubtful. Robison was never able to furnish proof of his purchase.

To further complicate the situation, the territorial legislature during its winter session in 1853-54 created a new county in the disputed area in an attempt to legitimize Young's influence.

According to affidavits received by Young, liquor was being supplied to local Indians on a regular basis from the fort's supplies. The northern Mormon settlements were too close to Fort Bridger to escape harm from drunken, armed Indians, according to Young.

Hickman's absence from the valley during the early summer of 1853 is attested to by the fact that two unclaimed letters waited for him and Bernetta at the Salt Lake Post Office. Hickman always picked up his mail when he was in the city. On 1 August, Hickman returned to Salt Lake City to report to Young, who, besides being president of the Mormon church and territorial governor, was also federal superintendent of Indian Affairs.

Young went to court and obtained a warrant, dated August 1853, from Judge Leonidas Shaver for the arrest of Bridger. Already called and ready to march to Fort Bridger was Sheriff James Ferguson. He and fifty battalion men had specific instructions from Daniel Wells to proceed to the Green River with presents to placate the Shoshones and "to arrest any and all persons engaged in furnishing Indians with guns and ammunition, including Jim Bridger." The letter further advised that Ferguson was to "take over any discovered guns and spill on the ground any and all spiritous liquors . . . and route out any lurking hostile Indians . . . taking care to preserve in your company order and decorum, cleanliness and sobriety." They were given permission to take a twelve-pound howitzer with them. Hickman was a member of Ferguson's "Minute Men."

Four days later, on 24 August 1853, Wells wrote to Lt. Col. William H. Kimball, requesting that he raise a second mounted corps of thirty men. Kimball was to muster these back-up troops and then try to join with Ferguson's men already en route to Fort Bridger. Wells warned Kimball to have his "men watch for ambush and to be extremely careful of animals and men, and to preserve cleanliness, and sobriety in camp."

They were told to "take all ammunition found, no matter who claimed it, and to search for Spiritious Liquors, and destroy all intended for Indian use, or for private use . . . Arrest and bring to Salt Lake City every offender against the laws and especially those who resisted the Sheriff Marshal."

Kimball raised a posse of forty-eight men, including Lott Huntington, son of Dimick B. Huntington, one of the Nauvoo Legion. Only nineteen years old in 1853, he would die nine years later at the hands of Orrin Porter Rockwell for horse stealing. Hickman mentions that he had known Huntington as a child.

Warned that the Mormons were on their way, Bridger fled the fort and, with the help of his Indian wife, hid in nearby willows. Bridger's words to Captain R. B. Marcy of the later federal expedition to Utah were that "'the Avenging Angels' of Brigham Young came to his place and forced him to escape to the woods." He successfully eluded the "Danites" and made his way to Fort Laramie, "leaving all his cattle and other property in possession of the Mormons."

From Fort Laramie Bridger returned to the United States and laid his case before authorities in Washington. Bridger would be employed as a guide in 1857 with the Utah expedition under Colonel Albert S. Johnston.

The autobiographies of Hickman, Ferguson, and Marcy confirm that Bridger had left when the Mormons arrived. Hickman doubted Bridger had gone to Laramie, but that was where he had fled, leaving the fort in the care of his partner Vasquez.

The Mormon expedition arrived at the fort in the evening of 26 August. General Lewis Robison was placed in charge of the contraband stores, "including four barrels, and a part of liquor, and 1 sack of powder, a large quantity of lead and balls, and a case of guns." About this time a Green River ferryman by the name of Elisha Ryan, acting in a "braggadocio manner," came to the fort leading a band of Shoshones. In a letter to Young, Sherriff Ferguson called Ryan "a dangerous man, who should not run at large." James S. Brown concurred: "Ryan has organized a war party to carry on his nefarious work of robbery."

Captain Robert T. Burton of the militia, later sheriff and constable of Salt Lake County and an avowed enemy of Hickman, attempted to arrest Ryan. Ryan resisted, but when his gang of Indians ran off in fear, he was easily taken into custody. His arrest was expected to serve as an example to others in the area, who were reported to Young "to be every day in their usual filth and drunkenness."

Hickman wrote to Young about the Mormon drunkenness at Fort Bridger, as the liquor stores were discovered and "destroyed in small doses." According to Hickman, the drinking was so heavy that he told Ferguson he was leaving. He was asked to take one of Ephraim Hanks's men with him. Hanks, he wrote, was "full of rum when they left." Four men, Hanks, Walker, Hickman, and Rufus Stoddard, left Fort Bridger on 28 August with prisoner Elisha

Ryan. Hickman liked Ryan. To Hickman, Ryan was an enterprising mountain man who usually got what he wanted.

At the first night's camp, Ryan escaped. Did Hickman help him, or were they all so "full of canteen" they were incapable of doing their job? Hickman returned to the valley without Ryan but unperturbed. Eleven days later he married his fifth wife, Hannah Diantha Horr, a seventeen-year-old who had arrived with an immigrant train during Hickman's stay at Fort Bridger.

Ferguson next ordered fifteen men to go to the Green River from Fort Bridger and arrest the mountain men. According to Hickman, they took enough liquor to last them until they got home. It is surprising that only two or three mountaineers were shot—the only casualties—given the number of drunken men fighting each other.

On 31 August, Young wrote to the combined forces of Ferguson and Kimball at the fort, reminding them that "the U.S. Marshal would hardly justify the seizing of Fort Bridger, except under the Indian laws, dependent upon proving Bridger had sold 'Spiritous Liquors' to the Indians." If proven, Bridger would be required "to forfeit his Fort, and all the stores within." Again came the unheeded warning: "Spill out all the liquor and take the guns and ammunition." Young suggested that thirty men be left at the fort during the winter or else "the villains will return and claim it." Louis Vasquez was still at the fort on 28 August when Ferguson referred to him as "Bridger's agent" and bought a beef from him.

A second letter from Young followed the first, advising Ferguson and Kimball to "leave the Fort undisturbed, except for confiscating the articles of contraband, namely, powder, lead, coffee, liquor, guns etc." Young hoped that by this quiet display of force, Bridger would be coerced to return and then be arrested.

Young wanted Green River County "Mormonized" and brought under his control. Bridger and Young could not both rule in Green River Country. One of them had to leave and Young knew he now held the upper hand. But Bridger on the run could mean unforetold difficulties in the east where he was becoming something of a folk hero and Young was increasingly seen as a lawless tyrant.

The fifteen men under the direction of Lewis Robison marched to the Green River ferries to show their authority and arrest resisters. Robison wrote to Ferguson on 31 August, requesting 100 pounds of beef, sugar, and coffee to feed his men—adding that he "can borrow flour from Capt. Crosbey's

Company." At the Green River ferries they found Elisha Ryan, who had reappeared there the day after his escape. Ryan succeeded in inciting a few mountain men to make a stand. Hickman writes that "Brigham had ordered Ryan killed if he did not come to terms."

Robison and thirty men remained at Fort Bridger during the winter, while the rest of the militia returned to Salt Lake City. Despite the presence of Robison and his men, by the end of 1853 the mountain men had retaken possession of all but one of the ferries. The mountaineers prepared to go to federal court in Salt Lake City to recover lost ferry fees, estimated at $30,000, which their competitor Hawley, Thompson & McDonald had received.

Hickman had already filed his own charges against Hawley, Thompson & McDonald for not paying him a finder's fee. He had been under contract with Hawley, Thompson & McDonald to ride throughout the Green River area and encourage immigrants to utilize the Mormon ferry. Court justices J. D. Little, Jedediah Grant, and Elias Smith awarded Hickman seventy dollars.

It is doubtful that Hickman solicited very much work for the ferry during the period under dispute. With a trading post sixty miles to the east, which yielded Hickman $9,000 in 1853, militia activity, and a marriage in August, he could not have rendered the "extensive" service he claimed. It appears that Hickman was never able to collect his seventy dollars.

At the October 1853 church conference, Young called Orson Hyde and John Nebeker to take thirty-nine men and Isaac Bullock to take fifty-three men to assault the fort. If they could not bring the fort under their control, they were to establish an independent supply settlement where Mormon wagon trains could be refurbished. This instruction led to the establishment of Fort Supply twelve miles southwest of Fort Bridger, a place Hosea Stout labeled, "The most forbidding and godforsaken place I have ever seen."

– 6 –

Return to Green River

In the spring of 1854 Bill Hickman left Salt Lake City in company with Mormon probate judge I. Appleby, Apostle Orson Hyde, Hosea Stout, George Hickman, George Boyd, and others. Although control of Fort Bridger and the Green River ferries was still in question, the Green River County was to be formally organized around Mormon settlements, with county officers appointed by Brigham Young. Probate judges like Appleby were usually Mormon bishops, with jurisdiction over crimes committed by Mormons and over domestic problems such as divorce. Appleby designated Hickman as sheriff of the new county. Hickman was also county assessor, tax collector, prosecuting attorney, and Utah territorial legislative representative. In addition, he was appointed a deputy U.S. marshal by federal marshal Joseph L. Heywood, an appointee of President Zachary Taylor. Hickman had additional instructions from Young to start a Mormon ferry for the use of Mormon settlers. Hyde was to preside over Fort Supply.

Three or four miles into East Canyon the party of new officials encountered Jesse T. Hartley, a young lawyer from Provo. Hickman describes Hartley as "a fine looking, intelligent young man," who had recently married a Miss Bullock of good family in Provo.

According to his autobiography, Hickman had heard reports that Young was critical of Hartley and that Young had preached against him. Hartley was originally from Oregon, where he apparently had a criminal record and had fled justice when he entered the Utah territory. Under false pretenses he had gone to Provo, where he had fallen in love with a young Mormon woman. To gain her father's permission for marriage, he had been baptized into the Mormon church, although it was later discovered that he was critical of the church in letters to friends in Oregon. Hartley was headed east, planning to abandon his wife and avoid criminal indictments from Oregon.

At least three warrants had been issued in Utah for Hartley's arrest for "forging drafts," stealing a horse, and avoiding trial. Hickman could have invited Hartley to come back with him to Salt Lake City to stand trial, or he could have allowed Hartley to escape into self-imposed exile. But Hickman claims Orson Hyde whispered to him, "Now is your time; don't let him come back." Whether Hartley was offered a choice nor not, he was shot through the head as he rode across a swollen stream in the mountains.

Hartley's Mormon wife, if Mormon apostate Ettie V. Smith can be believed, never forgave Hickman for killing her husband and leaving her with a "fatherless babe." Supposedly Hartley had told his wife he was afraid "he would be killed in the Endowment House in the Temple, because the Prophet required an atonement for sins such as his." The story of Hartley's death filled anti-Mormon writings for a generation, thanks to Ettie Smith's *Fifteen Years Among The Mormons*.

Hickman had spent the winter months of 1853-54 reading law. He successfully passed the bar examination in Salt Lake City, after "a pretty rigid examination." This was apparently his qualification for holding most of the appointed governing offices in Green River County. To look the part of a government official, Hickman had purchased a suit of black broadcloth, a white shirt, and a tie.

Hickman sent his brother George on to Pacific Springs to set up a trading post on the trail while he stayed in Green River and tried to win the ferrymen over to a peaceful compromise. Elisha Ryan was still encouraging other mountain men to defend their holdings and to sabotage competitors' ferries. They hijacked a ferry at Kinny's Point by cutting the mooring line. Judge Appleby issued a writ of arrest. Hickman took a posse of six men, including Mormon ferry owners Russell and Shockley, and started after Ryan. When they arrived at Kinny Point, where one of the ferries was located, they found Ryan in a drunken sleep. When he sobered up, he relinquished the ferry and the money he had collected and then fell asleep again.

On Saturday, 27 May, Hickman set out with non-Mormon ferry owner Captain William Hawley for Ham's Fork, where Hawley had agreed to operate his skiff for Mormon immigrants. The location came to be known as "Mormon Crossing" or "Mormon Ferry."

In 1856, William Hawley would be forced to sue John Russell, Fell Russell, J. H. Jones, and John Kerr of the Green River Ferry Company, his former partners, for "Demand and Damages" of $4,407.83. Apparently Hawley had invested heavily in three of the ferries, the Cherokee, the Kinny, and the Mormon, and had used Hickman as a supplier of immigrants to cross on his ferries. Hickman, who owned a 25 percent interest in the ferry, also sued Hawley to recover monies he claimed Hawley owed him. If either Hawley or Hickman collected on their suits, there is no record of a payment.

The Mormons secured Fort Bridger and started building a stone wall around it. Vestiges of this stone wall are all that remain today of the Mormon renovation of the fort.

Before the summer was over, Hickman's diplomacy had accomplished what the previous year's fighting had failed to do. The mountaineers, including a colorful man named Jack Robinson, agreed to peaceful co-existence, something that appeared impossible even a year before. Most of the old settlers were happy to have a semblance of order and government in the area. The Indians also became more friendly. Hickman says they recognized him as "a medicine man," especially after he made them presents.

It was a comfortable summer. Bernetta came to visit in June and stayed at least through 6 July. Hickman was busy with legal cases. A 29 May law suit before Judge Appleby over the estate of M. Caldwell, deceased, was apparently the first case Hickman tried in court. He represented John H. Bigler, the plaintiff suing for recovery of a mare. Hosea Stout represented the defense. Appleby's decision was "no cause for action."

Hickman was also Brigham Young's eyes and ears in the county. In mid-July he sent the following letter:

> Dear Bro. Brigham Young,
> By request of Bro. Appleby and others of the brethren here, I address you a line of information concerning affairs

in this country. We have used every exertion to lay all excitement and bad feelings that has existed amongst the Indians and mountaineers which we have successfully done. It has been no small job to do this. We have had to use much stratogm. We have not failed in anything which we have undertaken to do with the Indians—in the first place we learned Ryan was East with a large portion of Indians. I was satisfied that it was best to see him. I therefore wrote him a letter with some flattery and at the same time learned the feelings of the Mountaineers, which I found with but very few exception to be good toward Ryan. Jack Robinson, who is the man of most influence, thought Ryan to be a good fellow, but high strung and [Robinson] would do what was rite, if he thought he [Ryan] would not be hurt, on informing him he would not, he then sent an Indian after him in a few days he [Ryan] came with rather bad feeling from his last fall treatment [arrest], he brought some of the chiefs with him who stated they had given Ryan Green River and as no treaty had been made with them for their lands, [Ryan] thought his right to be good, but if it was not, he did not want it.

To settle this I advised him to compromise by . . . leaving it to Washington, which he readily consented to, and accordingly has done, binding himself to keep peace, and use his influence amongst the Indians to that effect—which [he] has done and continues to do. He talks much to the Indians in favor of the Mormons. He seems to take an interest in it. He will do anything I tell him and boast of it, for I am his friend, as he says he wants peace and will do anything, for us to affect it.

He is one of the Chiefs of the Shoshones and they consider him one of them and so do they think of all the Mountaineers who have *squaws for wives.* Jack Robinson tell[s] him to mind me and he will get along well. The Mountaineers all feel well. They say there has never been as good feelings here as now exists—there are many of them who are the greatest of scamps but are as good to us as they can be. I do not know of a man on the River but what would come at a word to assist me in arresting any person. They many times came and offer their services, and send word if I have anything to do with a large train, just call on them.

We have affected these feelings by telling them there is good feeling toward them, and none will be robbed. That some Mormons talk and act foolishly but not to mind it—this we had to do to get the good feeling of the Indians, for they were so linked together we had not power to separate them.

They are now working for us with the Indians, and will continue no doubt if some fool don't rip up what has been done. Porter Rockwell is very anxious to do it. He says he don't care for what has been done. If he could find the Indians he would do as he was a mind to. We have talked to Bro. George Bean, he sees how things are here. He sees as we do and is satisfied, and as we have taken much pains in explaining to him I wish you would converse with him as he can give you satisfaction on anything I have not.

Bro. Appleby, Brown, and myself have acted together and been agreed in all that has been done. We look at things alike.

The Indians want to know what will be given them for their lands and what is going to be done for them. This is all they wish to know at this time. They feel well and are coming in to see you as soon as corn and melons ripe, and have a feast, and also some of the Mountaineers who have squaws with them. Ryan wished me to write to you that he would be a good man and use every exertion to make the Indians good and do just what you said.

As ever, W. A. Hickman

There are many things I would like to talk with you about concerning affairs in this country. The Indians wish a trading post established on their lands near the buffalos, so they can trade, and have something to eat at the same time. They want it on Snake River. Jack Robinson says it is a good place to raise grain, and if we will make a settlement he will go with us so he can educate his [Indian] children. He wished me to talk with you about it, but he need[s] the rite kind of a man to keep a [trading] post.

James S. Brown records in his autobiography, "I saw Wm. A. Hickman at Green River in the year 1854. He was sheriff at this time. I found him cunning in his official work and always ready to support the law, blood would have been shed more than once but for him."

Hickman had always found Ryan sympathetic and found him a great help during three trips to the Shoshone tribe, because Ryan spoke Shoshonean. Ryan came to Salt Lake City with Hickman to see Brigham Young. Young told him to be patient because he would get his money back the next year on the ferries that were no longer his. Ryan asked for a loan of between $500 and $1,000. Young declined but turned to Hickman and suggested he arrange a loan for his friend. Hickman says he borrowed $750.

On 5 December 1854, D. B. Huntington filed a report to the *Deseret News* from Ogden, reporting that "Major David Moore has complained about Indians south of Ogden killing calves and burning fence poles." The next day, "Wm. A. Hickman and Elisha Ryan were picked as the leaders for 8 or 10 citizens, at Brigham's bidding, to go in 3 or 5 wagons to meet the Utah Indians." Ryan was proving to be of worth to the Mormons as an interpreter. But in the spring of 1855 he was shot and killed at Fort Bridger by a Spaniard named "Joe" for no apparent reason. The assailant escaped. Hickman was left to repay the $750 loan from his own funds.

Hickman also wrote of a trip into the Wind River Mountains with four companions, two of them Indians. They traveled Indian style, meaning they had no supplies. The five almost starved on the eight-day march. The Indians finally shot an antelope, which the famished men roasted and gorged on before falling asleep.

This trip was followed by an altercation, which ended in another court case on 20 October 1854. Hosea Stout, Hickman's frequent legal confederate and partner, described this episode in some detail. A man named Twitchell stole eleven horses. The federal marshal (probably Heywood) recovered the horses and placed them in the yard of one B. Hawkes for safe-keeping. Twitchell, the thief, found the horses and sold four of them to Levi Abrams, "a mean and contemptible Jew" according to Stout. Abrams put them in his stable and refused to surrender them to Judge Burton when requested to do so. Burton called Hickman to recover the horses. Hickman and Abrams got into a bloody fight, after which Abrams went to court and swore out a complaint against Hickman, alleging that "he had drawn a knife and also a club, with intent to kill him." Hickman was arrested, and Hosea Stout, Jesse Little, and Albert Carrington (later a Mormon apostle) handled his defense. On hearing the evidence, Judge Shaver discharged Hickman.

For the winter, Lewis Robison was left in charge of Fort Bridger, under the absentee direction of James Brown. In his diary for 11 June 1854, Hosea Stout mentioned that the Mormons purchased the fort from Vasquez some time before. Perhaps Robison made a private deal with Vasquez to buy the fort even though Jim Bridger had not yet returned from the east. Years later

Robison would file a lawsuit against the U.S. government, claiming that he was the rightful owner of the fort. But at this point the Mormons apparently felt that the Mormon church owned the fort.

– 7 –

Fort Bridger and Margaret

Hickman was still involved with the ferry business on the Green River in 1855. James S. Brown wrote, "Having acquired a fourth interest in three ferries on Green River, I arranged with my 3 partners, Isaac Bullock, Lewis Robison, and Wm. Hickman, so that I did not have to go there as my health was not very good, hence I remained in Ogden." Hickman's account was that he "bought a fourth interest in the ferries; went to Green River, repaired the boats, and got the ferries in running condition."

Most Utah chroniclers remember 1855 as "a grasshopper year." Hickman mentions the devastation. "The grass on the benches look[ed] burnt," he wrote. Because of this, it was anticipated that spring immigration would be light. So Hickman, in company with several others, including his "hired men," decided to prospect for gold again, this time along the Sweetwater River in the South Pass region of the high plains area of present-day Wyoming and further east in the Wind River ranges. This is the first mention of "hired men"—no doubt the beginning of what would evolve into "his gang," which by 1859 was rumored to consist of a "large band of outlaws."

The prospecting party found mountain lakes surrounded by immense snow beds and abundant wild life. The group climbed Fremont Peak and went on into even higher areas. Hickman says he laughed when he remembered that some had thought Fremont Peak was America's highest mountain. They found gold in every stream but of poor quality. Hickman returned home, stayed a few days, and returned to Green River to run for the territorial legislature, which still met in Fillmore, Utah.

On 28 March, about two months prior to his trip, Hickman married again—this time to two women in one day. The first, Sarah Elizabeth Johnson, was the daughter of his good friend, Luke Johnson. The other was a Shoshone Indian named Margaret, reportedly a servant of Brigham Young. Young performed both marriages in the Endowment House, and both marriages appear to have been arranged. Sarah was reportedly the first of Hickman's plural wives considered to be as attractive as Bernetta. Her beauty would later be the cause of trouble in the Hickman household. Sarah was also twenty-six years old, past her prime according to Hickman's standards. She bore Bill five children.

Brigham Young may have kept in mind Hickman's 1854 letter describing the advantages of negotiators taking "Indian squaws for wives." Why not Margaret, a woman of thirty-five who worked in Young's home? Hickman probably would have chosen a younger squaw. But eighteen months later this marriage would help Hickman make peace with the Shoshone tribe. In the meantime Margaret sewed and beaded magnificent matching buckskin suits for herself and her new husband.

Near the end of July, Jim Bridger returned from the east to rejoin his business partner Louis Vasquez and to reclaim his fort. Bridger found Lewis Robison operating the fort and Vasquez working as a storekeeper. He also found Bill Hickman, who had just arrived from the Green River ferries.

Robison recommended that Bridger sell the fort to the Mormons. Bridger noted the improvements that had been made since he left and the general feelings of peace in the area and refused to sell. On Tuesday, 31 July, Robison left Fort Bridger for Fort Supply twelve miles away. Apparently he felt that Hickman might accomplish more toward the sale if left alone with Bridger.

Hickman did persuade Bridger to sell, but Bridger asked $8,000—a price he apparently believed the Mormons would never be able to pay. On Wednesday, 1 August, Hickman left for Fort Supply to talk with Robison. On Thursday, Robison and Hickman returned to Fort Bridger, bringing with them a load of gold worth $4,000. They surprised Bridger by accepting his price and agreeing to pay $4,000 down with the balance due in fifteen months. Bridger and Vasquez both placed their marks on a sales agreement and acknowledged receipt of the first payment.

On 12 October 1855 the *Deseret News* printed a letter to Hickman from George A. Boyd at Fort Bridger: "We learn that the Indians are constantly killing cattle, both those belonging to the Fort ranches, and to the Mountaineers. There is a report on a wagon train led by Brother Andrus at Green River that can't roll because of lack of supplies and the destitute condition of the travelers." Hickman had returned to Salt Lake City in early October, where he was involved, usually as a defense attorney, in several lawsuits.

The territorial legislature convened in Fillmore, Utah, on 10 December 1855. Hickman had been elected Green River County representative that August. According to Brigham Young's records, "All were present except W. A. Hickman." The following day, Hickman arrived, rented a room, had it furnished, and dressed in his best clothes. He served for forty days and was named to the Committee of Counties and Corporations.

Hickman introduced Act H. F. No. 14 on 17 December, which was passed on 22 December, granting all of Rush Valley to Brigham Young, Wilford Woodruff, Luke Johnson, James W. Cummings, Samuel Bennion, William A. Hickman, Jesse C. Little, and Claudius V. Spencer to use as "herd ground." Only an elite few received large grants of "herd land." Hickman evidently saw an opportunity to control Rush Valley. When overseeing the church's herds, he had built a house there, where Minerva lived. A month later, on 11 January 1856, he introduced a bill requesting the creation of Shambip County, which would include Rush Valley and would run south to Juab County. This was approved. Luke Johnson was chosen as probate judge for the county, and George Hickman the notary public. However, by 1860 Shambip County still showed a population of only 162. Luke Johnson died the following year, and all county records and books of administration were turned over to Tooele County.

During this legislative session, Hickman joined the chorus of denunciations against Judge W. W. Drummond, a federal appointee to the district court. Drummond had allegedly abandoned his wife and children in Washington, D.C., before accepting the judicial appointment in Utah territory. In his wife's place he brought a mistress from Baltimore, who would sit on the bench and pass notes to the judge while court was in session. Hickman heard about this in Salt Lake City on his way from Green River to Fillmore. He said if he had a case to present in Drummond's court and his paramour was there, he would kick them both out. Drummond heard of this threat and swore out a writ for Hickman's arrest. Hickman let it be known around Fillmore that if the writ were served, he would "horsewhip the judge."

Hickman persuaded Levi Abrams of Green River County to file charges against the judge. The case was brought to court, and Hickman took full advantage of the opportunity to denounce and humiliate Drummond before Abrams withdrew his complaints four days into the trial. Drummond was infuriated. "We were never friends afterwards," Hickman later commented.

At the end of the legislative session, Hickman and Hosea Stout, who would work with Hickman on a number of cases between 1854 and 1859, returned to their homes in Taylorsville and Salt Lake City. Hickman had already made an unscheduled stop in Taylorsville on his way to the legislative session, which was why he was a day late. Two of his wives, Sarah Basford Meacham and Diana Case, bore him children nine months after he was counted absent in Fillmore.

Hickman calls 1856 a year of "no great interest." The immigration of pioneers into the valley was small, but according to Hickman crops were good and all had enough to eat. However, 1856 was the year the Willie and Martin Handcart Companies arrived in the valley. Hickman helped to rescue these men and women from early snowdrifts in Wyoming.

The summer months, May to mid-September, were spent on the Green River. While Hickman was there in 1856, a humorous drama unfolded among the Hickman wives living in Taylorsville. According to Hickman's granddaughter, Marie Kohlhepp Nash, Bernetta, then forty-six years old, feigned a pregnancy. Bernetta had stopped having babies about the time the younger wives were beginning their families. She had become a mother figure to the younger women, who always called her "gramma." During the winter and spring of 1856-57, seven of Hickman's younger wives were expecting babies, all within one eighteen-month period. Bernetta reportedly began wrapping and stuffing extra clothing around her middle, adding rags each month to increase her stomach's size. She continued in this condition for eleven months until she confided in Minerva, the third wife, who disappeared with Bernetta to the barn where they gave birth to her "rag baby." Bernetta then spent two weeks in bed to recover from the "death" of her baby, "buried behind the barn," and the promise that no one would ever tell Hickman.

FORT BRIDGER AND MARGARET

Another story that must date from this same period was told to one of Hickman's grandsons in 1919 by eighty-one-year-old George Goodhart:

> The first time I ever met your grandfather, he, Port Rockwell and Lot Smith were camped on Green River. At that time I was a boy working for the American Fur Company. I was sent with a message to some of the trappers some distance away. Not finding them at night I came across some gentle horses. I got down and examined the hobbles and could tell they belonged to white men. . . . I got on my horse again, and could see a fire. I called, 'Hello, White Men's friend,' and they answered and told me to come around and camp with them. One piloted me into camp; he took my horse and put it with theirs. They had a kettle of venison on the fire, the finest I ever ate. After supper I told them how glad I was not to have come across any of them damn Mormons. They asked me why. I told them that the Mormons killed people on sight, murdered the emigrants, and that I was more afraid of them than of the savage Indians. Port and Lot slept together, I slept with Hickman. Next morning, one of them gathered the horses, and at breakfast I told them some Mormons had been seen in that vicinity.
>
> After breakfast I saddled my horse, then Hickman said to me, 'How have we treated you?' I told him, 'fine.' I could not have been treated better and said how pleased I was to have found them. Then he said, 'Tell your company we treated you to the best we had and we are all Mormons and that we are Port Rockwell, Lot Smith, and Bill Hickman.' My heart seemed to jump to my mouth. I never was so scared in all my life. I touched my horse with a spur and as soon as I was through the brush, I leaned over and ran my horse as fast as he'd go. I expected to be shot every minute, but no shot came.

A third anecdote from this period was Hickman's youngest daughter's favorite story about her father:

> Two young brothers who had been out with their sheep all day came into town in the evening to a large celebration, the climax of which was a dance. The boys felt they could not go into the dance because they didn't have any shoes or what they did have were entirely too shabby to dance in. They decided to sit on the fence outside the dance hall and enjoy the merriment inside vicariously. Bill Hickman came along and asked them why they were sitting on the fence and not

inside dancing. When he learned the reason he said, 'I'll sit on the fence while you young boys go in there taking turns using my boots,' which they proceeded to do for several hours.

The Indians in 1856 were still twelve years from settlement on reservations, and they and the Mormon settlers continued to fight. As the northern territorial Indian problem continued in the summer of 1856, Brigham Young asked Hickman to seek out Chief Washakie, by now the most prominent chief of the Shoshone, and show him the benefits of civilization. Hickman, as Young's mouthpiece, invited the Indians to Fort Bridger. At his side were Lewis Robison and Isaac Bullock.

On 19 August 1856, Hickman and his Indian wife Margaret, both dressed in their beaded-buckskin suits, met with forty lodges of Indians (numbering about three hundred). Gifts were distributed. The Indians believed Young had supplied the gifts, when they were in fact presents from the U.S. government. The Indians showed great friendliness to Hickman and his associates.

Hickman was back in Taylorsville by summer's end. Bishop John Bennion recorded: "September 26, 1856: wrote a note to J. Macky to help Hickman make a bowery for the military party." The Mormon milita was beginning to practice regularly. On 28 September, Bennion added: "Did military duty at Fort Hickman."

Troubled times were ahead. On 3 October 1856, W. M. F. McGraw, superintendent of the South Pass Wagon Road, wrote to President Zachary Taylor in Washington, D.C.:

> No vestige of law and order left . . . An ecclesiastical organization, as despotic, dangerous and damnable, as has ever been known to exist in the country . . . running not only those who do not subscribe to their religious code, but is driving the moderate and more orderly Mormon community to desperation . . . whose laws, or rather conspiracies, are framed in dark corners, promulgated from the stand of Tabernacle or Church, executed at midnight, or upon the highways, by an organized band of braves and assassins whose masters compel an outraged community to tolerate.

On 10 October 1856, Hickman appeared before a grand jury with six others, including Hosea Stout, "to answer such questions as might be put to them by said Grand Jury, in relating to offenses committed against the laws of the Territory of Utah."

Elias Smith, the Mormon judge who presided over the hearing, was anxious to allay fears in Washington, D.C., that the territory was out of control without actually bringing charges against anyone. Ten days later, a letter in the church-owned *Deseret News* by "a late citizen of Utah" repeated one of the incidents being considered by the grand jury:

> That one Joseph Traskolowski, a government officer, was knocked down and beat in the streets and the perpetrators not brought to justice, but suffered to roam at large: that the *notorious* Bill Hickman, that assisted to do the deed, a few days after, was sent to the Snake Indians, with a load of Indian goods, instead of the agent Armstrong.

The anonymous author then added that many of the Gentiles in Utah were "infernal scoundrels, who come cursing and damning the Mormons," and who probably deserved the treatment they received from the Mormons.

The epithet "The Notorious" was applied to Hickman for the first time in this letter. Hickman evidently accepted it as a kind of badge of honor—and fear—and would even be remembered as "The Notorious" in his obituary twenty-seven years later.

– 8 –

Brigham's Mailman

Two events marked 1857 as a major turning point both in the history of the Utah territory and the life of Bill Hickman: the BYX Company and the Mormon War. Also, the "Mormon Reformation" was in full swing by 1857. This period of religious fervor began two years earlier during the "grasshopper year," when clouds of insects had swarmed from the Wasatch Mountains into the Salt Lake Valley, washing up four feet high around the Great Salt Lake. Then came months of drought and a severe winter, during which the church's herd of 2,000 cattle was reduced to 420. One-half of all cattle in the territory died from starvation or froze to death. People ate weeds to survive. "Fast Day" was instituted on the first Thursday of every month to help ration the food supply and to turn the Saints in their hardships towards God.

In the midst of these troubles, Brigham Young called Bill Hickman to be a mailman for his new Brigham Young Express Freight and Mail Company. Back in December 1845, Young had written from Nauvoo to William L. Marcy, United States secretary of war, requesting funds to build stockades and block houses between Illinois and the Rocky Mountains and to establish a mail route between the two areas.

Mail service was the only regular contact western settlements had with the outside world before the telegraph reached the intermountain area in 1861, and there was fierce competition for the mail contract awarded from Washington. The 1,200-mile mail route from Independence, Missouri, to Salt Lake City was known as the Central Route. This link was threatened during the 1850s by a succession of failures, as contractors with the government went bankrupt or tried to operate on a shoe-string and were forced to sell.

Mormons had their own mail-carriers from 1851 to 1853: Ephraim Hanks, Feramorz Little (a nephew of Brigham Young), and Charles F. Decker. One contemporary recalled, "They frequently swam rivers with mail bags on their heads, or formed floats of Indian-Rubber bed sacks . . . They sometimes carried 24 heavy bags of mail for the Great Salt Lake." The men met at Fort Laramie on the 15th of each month. From there they traveled 400 miles to Fort Bridger without a way-station until the Devil's Gate station was established.

Samuel H. Woodson held the first contract with the federal government between 1850 and 1854, for which he received $19,500 a year. Beginning 1 July 1854, a new contract for a monthly service was let to William M. F. McGraw and John E. Reeside for $36,000. McGraw was on good terms with U.S. president Zachary Taylor, which may explain why he was offered the contract in the first place. On 3 October 1856 he wrote to the president complaining about the Mormons. His observations helped produce the military orders for a "Utah Expedition." Garland Hart, a federal Indian agent stationed in Utah, had also written letters to President Taylor, and his letters probably contributed to President James Buchanan's decisions about Utah after he took office on 3 March 1857.

Before writing his inflammatory letter, McGraw had managed to establish six of the twelve proposed relay stations on the mail route: Big Blue River (Marysville, Kansas); Fort Kearney, Nebraska; Ash Hollow, below Fort Laramie (where the trail crossed to the North Platte); Fort Laramie, in what would later be eastern Wyoming territory; Independence Rock (on the lower Sweetwater); and Fort Bridger in the Utah territory. The same crew was to travel the full 1,200 miles with one light mule wagon for passengers and another for the mail bags.

Heavy snow and Indian problems in Wyoming blocked passenger and mail service to Salt Lake City in the winter of 1854-55. Still service on the McGraw-Hockaday line recommenced in August 1855. (Reeside had withdrawn from the mail contract in late 1854, and John Hockaday, a Salt Lake City lawyer interested in overland transportation systems, had stepped in to fill Reeside's absence.) Revenues were up, but by year's end

McGraw decided he wanted out. When this news reached Young, he was quick to put in a bid for the new contract for 1855-56. Plans were made for new way stations and a regular service using Mormon riders.

On 19 October 1856, U.S. postmaster general James Campbell awarded the mail contract to Hiram Kimball, representing Brigham Young's newly formed BYX Company, for $23,000. The company name had been reduced to initials to conceal Young's involvement. Kimball and Young did not learn of their good fortune for some time because of a delay in the mail. This delay postponed the first BYX mail departure from the valley until 8 February 1857.

As the first departure date approached, Young asked Hickman and Orrin Porter Rockwell to be his chief mailmen. Rockwell was to carry the mail from Salt Lake City to Fort Bridger, and Hickman from Fort Bridger to Independence, Missouri. On 6 February, Young's office journal reported: "Instructed Hickman on how to carry the Mail."

Hickman did not want the job. In winter the trip would be horrendous—only two weeks earlier a rider had frozen to death in East Canyon. But Young persuaded Hickman it was his duty to go, and he reluctantly agreed to make the trip. He knew he would be gone almost four months at a time. In his book he laments that he arrived back in the valley in late June $1,000 poorer than when he departed. He was never paid for his part in the project.

On 5 February Young wrote to his nephew Feramorz Little expressing his confidence in Hickman and advising Little that Hickman was to determine the value of McGraw's animals, since the church was considering purchasing them. Young wrote to Apostle Orson Pratt in Europe: "The mail to the East will be carried out this time by Wm. A. Hickman and others, and . . . [we will later] add an express and carrying company, for freight, passengers, etc."

That Hickman completed this assignment is evident in a 1 March letter from Brigham Young to Orson Pratt: "On the 8th of last month we sent out the first mail eastward, in charge of 8 men, W. A. Hickman, conductor." John Bennion also noted: "February 8, 1857: Very cold day. Hickman started east with B.Y.X. mail."

Several things happened to make the trip memorable. First was the well publicized departure on 8 February from the south gate of Temple Square. Just minutes before his departure, hands were laid on Hickman's head and he was given a blessing by church patriarch, John Young:

> You shall have wives and children and your posterity shall be exceedingly numerous upon the earth and your words shall be a law unto your family. You shall have power to govern and control yourself and all whom you are set to control and to govern . . . You shall have power over all your enemies, even to set your feet upon their necks, and no weapon that is formed against you shall prosper, in as much as your heart is set to keep the commandments . . . Thou shall be blest in flocks and herds, and in all that thou puttest thy hands to do. I bless you with health, strength, and life and say thy body shall be blest with health . . . to perform the duties, the arduous duties you shall have to perform.
>
> You shall have wisdom, discretion, and understanding and knowledge to foresee evil, when danger approaches you the Angel of Life shall be with you to forewarn you of those things. If you are faithful you shall assist in avenging the blood of the prophets of God, and assist in accomplishing the great work of the last days . . . You shall be blest in all things and not a hair of your head shall fall to the ground by the enemy . . . [God] shall give you favor in the eyes of the people where you are going and you shall fill your mission with honor and return safe to the valleys of the mountains, to your family and friends. The Angel of mercy and life shall be upon your right hand in all times of trouble, danger and difficulty, and trial, and everything shall fall before you that might be used to prevent you from accom-plishing the duties of life.

Young watched as Hickman and Rockwell departed on that cold day with their companions: Joshua Terry, John Black, Charles Woodard, Heber Woodard, George Boyd, and William Henefer. They were also accompanied by "Monty" Jack, a California gambler heading east who wanted to make it over the mountains.

Hickman's fears about the journey were not unfounded. He was forty-two years old, the father of thirteen children, one to be born a week after he left, and husband to nine wives. In August 1856 he had married Mary Lucretia Horr, age twenty-one, a sister to Hannah Diantha Horr, and in November 1856 Martha Diana Case, age thirty-three, a recently widowed school teacher with four children.

During this first mail trip, Hickman's horse plowed through snowdrifts up to its belly as he crossed the mountains between

Utah and Wyoming. Hickman and his group took a month to reach Devil's Gate, one of the BYX Company way stations. Inside they found twenty men at the end of their rations, the snow so deep the men could not go east or west for supplies. The man in charge was a fellow Missourian, Dan Jones. He and his men had eaten scraps from their worn-out moccasins, spiced with a chunk of buffalo hide that previously had served as doormat. All that was left for a last stew was a pack saddle when Hickman arrived at the door with buffalo meat. He stayed a day then left two mules with the men. Although there was a food storage hut nearby, with supplies for the mail carriers, the men had been afraid to break in and eat. Hickman called them "foolish," opened the storage cabin, and all ate heartily.

Ten days later Hickman was at Fort Laramie, the half-way point to his destination. There the land was flat and dry and still covered with buffalo herds. One of his men tried to lasso a buffalo and was nearly killed, as they tumbled head over heels behind the buffalo until the rope broke. After a few days' rest, Hickman and the others started for Independence, reaching their destination two months and three days after having left Salt Lake City.

On 25 February 1857 the *Deseret News* had reported: "*Eastern Mail*: Nothing has been heard of the mail from the East since Mr. Gerrish left it a long time ago at the Platte Bridge. True to uniform, imbecile and reckless course the late contractor McGraw does not appear to care a farthing about completing his contract . . . As noticed at the time, Mr. Hickman started early in February with the first mail under the new contract. Mr. Groesbeck will start on March 2 and soon the route will be amply supplied with energetic men and plenty of animals."

Under the date of 13 April 1857, Young recorded the following in his journal:

> Brother Mumford arrived from Ft. Supply—first news from beyond Green River since November to the end of February.
>
> Mail with Hickman did not arrive at Ft. Supply until Mar. 6, [it required 26 days to go 90 miles, the snow was so deep]. Hickman left [Fort Supply], on the 8th of March. Orrin P. Rockwell past by Ft. Supply on March 27th. The delay of mail from Independence now solved. Bro. Hickman could hardly reach Independence in time to bring back

April 1mail, if he only left on March 8—so we can't expect mail until 1st of June.

Hickman crossed the state of Missouri by floating down the Missouri River. From Boonesville he telegraphed Washington, D.C., that the mail was delivered, and then he headed northeast to Adair County to visit his parents, who had moved there in 1849. This was his first trip home in thirteen years. It would also be his last. Hickman's father lived until August 1888. His mother would pass away in December 1877. Both were buried on their farm. Hickman also found that his brother George W. had returned to Missouri from Utah. Bill persuaded him to come back to the Rockies. Later Bill would also visit his in-laws in Randolph County to the south and his brother Thomas in St. Joseph, Missouri.

Hickman's visits with his family were short because he was scheduled to start back soon with the territory mail. Apparently he arrived a few days late, and the largest load of mail was given to Ephraim Hanks, an old mail hand. Hanks arrived in the valley with eight sacks of mail on 23 June. On that day, Young's journal notes: "Eight sacks of mail arrived at 2:15 p.m. 23 days from Independence—with Ephraim K. Hanks, who left Independence on June 1."

Hickman would arrive in the valley the next day. He picked up the three days of accumulated mail and traveled to Laramie, where he and two of his men decided to race to the valley. They traveled the entire five hundred miles in six-and-a-half days, eighty-one miles per day on horseback. Young noted Hickman's arrival: "Elder William A. Hickman arrived from the frontiers."

On 10 June 1857 U.S. president James Buchanan had decided to cancel the BYX mail contract. Buchanan had read reports from federal officials mailed from the valley during the winter which, ironically, were probably carried east in Hickman's mail sacks on 8 February 1857. In addition, in the spring of 1857, several judges, including Drummond, arrived in Washington with further tales of mistreatment. Federal authorities became convinced Brigham Young's aim was to set up an independent state. The way to strike back was first to cancel the Mormons' mail contract. Young had spent $125,000 establishing the BYX Mail Co. but would never receive any payment from the government. For political reasons, Buchanan decided on a southern route for the the mail to California, and the Salt Lake contract was let to Stephan B. Miles of Delaware for $32,000.

In an editorial published on 7 October 1857, the *Deseret News* summed up these recent events: "Utah from its first settlement has been imposed upon by mail contractors. The Post Office took away the contract after the mail was carried speedily, regularly, and safely." Two months later, on 9 December, the following notice appeared in the paper:

> All persons who furnished horses, mules, wagons, harnesses or other description of property to the B.Y.X. Co. are requested to appear, personally or by agent, at the Church cattle yard in Great Salt Lake City on Saturday the 19th when the animals and other private property in the possession of said Co. will be turned over to the several rightful claimants . . . that the late B.Y.X. Co. may be enabled to close the accounts.

The reason Hickman had hurried back to the valley was that he had heard government troops were preparing to come to Utah. According to Hickman, Young laughed at the warning. Young's own journal recorded simply, "Friday, June 26th, 1857: Spent the forenoon with Brother Hickman who arrived yesterday from the States." Hickman's warning came a month before July 24, the date traditionally assigned to the first report of approaching troops.

Hickman visited Young before he went home to see his family in Taylorsville. His visit home is confirmed by the births nine months later of Luke Johnson Hickman, born on 1 March 1858 to Sarah Elizabeth, and Margaret Rose Hickman, born on 13 March 1858 to Minerva.

By August, Young was taking the approaching army seriously. On 5 August, he proclaimed martial law in the territory, a first step toward war. Young asked Hickman to go to the Green River to check on developments there, and on August 23, Hickman wrote to Young, using the salutation "Scout":

Scout

Brother B. Young

> I have this morning come to this place having been to the mail station on Sweetwater. On the knight of the 20th. I was at Sweetwater, seen Bro. Markham about midnight— Stewart's [identity not known] train was there, one Co. [of] Mormons and a handcart Co. close by as per report of some

person who had been a short distance back on the road—McGraws Co. who had been in the mountains was there also.

All of the companies and Markham also going to leave the morning of the 21. Their stock, Jews and Gentiles all mixed up. I see them driving in every direction—Magraws men going to Baker's ferry on Green River where the balance of their men and animals were at which place they were going to remain till Magraw comes—they were to be there in 5 days from that time going round up Sweetwater to take in some waggon's etc. I will leave here day after tomorrow.

As ever Wm. A. Hickman

– 9 –

The Utah War

On 16 July 1857, part of the U.S. Army stationed at Fort Leavenworth received orders to march to Utah territory, assist in removing Brigham Young from office, and to replace him as governor with Alfred Cumming.

Plans for the Utah expedition had been made as early as 28 May, when the following circular was issued at army headquarters:

> [H]aste for the assemblage of a body of troops at Fort Leavenworth thence to Utah as soon as assembled. Instructions: 1. 2d dragoons, 5th Infantry, 10th Inf. & Phelph's battery of 4th Artillery, not less than 2500 men. plus medical officers. About 2000 head of beef cattle, 6 mo. supply of bacon (for 2 days in a week), and desicated vegetables for health of the troops in coming winter.—storage tents, stoves, enough for at least the sick.

In August a letter from the war department to Colonel Albert S. Johnston of the Second Cavalry, Washington, D.C., inducted him into the campaign. Two weeks after Johnston received his orders, he was ready to march on Utah. He was to ride ahead with an advance party, while the bulk of the troops was expected to require two months to make the trek. Johnston wrote:

> September 16, 1857, Head Quarters, Army of Utah—Ft. Leavenworth: Six companies of the 2d Dragoons under command of Col. Cooke prepared to march to Utah . . . charged with duty of escorting the Governor (Col. Cumming), and the civil officers of that Territory to Salt Lake City . . . he (Col. Cooke) may be expected to arrive in the

> Valley of Utah by the 15th or 20th of November.... as soon as I see Col. Cooke's command on the route I will also leave for Salt Lake City with an escort of 40 men detached from the Dragoons—I may be expected at place of destination the 20th of October . . . need to build suitable quarters for the troops by the ensuing winter.

The following day, 17 September, Johnston left Fort Leavenworth.

The decade of isolation Brigham Young had prayed for was coming to a close. James Henry Martineau, adjutant of one of the Mormon military districts in Utah, wrote, "At this time [1857], a state of War virtually existed in Utah. No travel was permitted in the Territory without a pass signed by Col. Dame, myself, or a Battalion Commander."

Brigham Young warned that he did not want any killing if it could be avoided. However, the Mormons were committed to fight rather than be dictated to by the federal government. "With God's help it would be a short war" was the way some would remember it.

An "express" system carrying messages to and from the mountains was in operation by the first week of August. Also in August Young called all outlying Saints back to Salt Lake City. Most complied. The 450 Carson Valley Saints, traveling in 123 wagons, left for Salt Lake City on 5 September 1857 and arrived on 2 November, by which time the first phase of the war was nearly over.

On 1 August George A. Smith, Young's counselor, headed south with military instructions for church leaders. Militia members south of Nephi were to be the church's second line of defense. The northern Utah men, being the first line, were the only ones required to leave their homes and families to position themselves in Echo Canyon as soldiers.

George A. Smith weighed over 300 pounds, but he managed a grueling itinerary as he delivered Young's messages. Smith probably carried with him a copy of Young's war proclamation:

> 1. To forbid, in the name of the people of the U.S. in the Territory of Utah, all armed forces, of every description from coming into this Territory, under any pretense whatsoever.
>
> 2. That all the forces in said Territory hold themselves in readiness to march, at a moments notice, to repel any and all such threatened invasion.

THE UTAH WAR 69

Martial law is hereby declared to exist in this Territory from and after the publication of this Proclamation and no person shall be allowed to pass or repass into, or through, or from this Territory without a permit from the proper officer.

Smith also carried the following letter from Daniel Wells, Mormon general in the field, to all militia leaders:

Sir:
The people of this Territory have lived in strict obedience to the laws of the parent and home government and are every [one] zealous for the supremacy of the constitution and the rights guaranteed thereby—they are not willing to endure longer these increasing outrages, but if an exterminating war be proposed against them and blood alone can cleanse pollution from the nations bullworks, . . . You are instructed to hold your command in readiness to march at the shortest possible notice to any part of the Territory. See that the law is strictly enforced in regard to arms and ammunition as far as practicable, that each ten (men), be provided with a good wagon and 4 horses or mules as well as necessary clothing etc. for a winter campaign.

Young feared movement of any kind through the territory, reasoning that spies could lead troops north from Santa Fe or east from Los Angeles and attack the territory from behind. Franklin McNeal tried to disobey the proclamation and was imprisoned for three or four months in Salt Lake City. He blamed Young and Wells for his internment and after the war attempted to sue them. He was shot and killed a year later in a personal feud with Joe Rhodes, an acquaintance of Bill Hickman. A group known as the Aiken Gang stumbled onto the Utah militia making preparations for war and were executed for violating Young's proclamation. Even an immigrant train, headed for California, was not allowed passage through the territory, the men being executed by zealous Mormons and Indians at Mountain Meadows in southern Utah.

The Aiken party consisted of six well-outfitted gamblers from the California gold fields who had entered the territory from the west intending to reach the U.S. Army troops near Fort Bridger. Soldiers were usually an easy "mark" for their gaming skills. The six were John Aiken, his brother Thomas, "Tuck" Wright, "Colonel" Erchad, Andrew J. "Honesty" Jones, and John Chapman. They were arrested by Major Smith of the Mormon militia in Box Elder County in early October and brought through Weber Canyon into Salt Lake City.

Four men had been appointed to escort the gang out of the territory—in the direction of San Bernadino. For some unknown reason, "Honesty" Jones and John Chapman had remained in Salt Lake City, "under guard" according to Hickman, "free" according to Hosea Stout. The four escort members appointed by Brigham Young were Orrin Porter Rockwell, John Lott, John Murdock, and Sylvanus Collett. Hosea Stout wrote in his diary on 20 November 1857: "O. P. Rockwell, and three or four others, start with 4 prisoners south, guarding for some days." He added, "The other 2 are going to be permitted to go at large and remain till spring and the guard dismissed."

According to later testimony, Thomas Aiken and "Colonel" Erchad were murdered by their escorts about 16 November at the first night's camp south of Nephi. John Aiken and Tuck Wright escaped but were severely wounded and dragged themselves back to Nephi. Two days later they were ambushed and drowned in the Mona Lakes. About 20 November, Jones discovered what had happened to his four traveling companions near Nephi and told all who would listen.

At that point, according to Hickman, Brigham Young had Hickman called to his office and told Hickman to get rid of this man, who was "making such a stink." Young allegedly said the man must be "used up." So Hickman, according to his autobiography, made arrangements with two of Young's "boys," William Kimball and George D. Grant, to put "Buck" Jones away—in a ditch with a hole in his head near Warm Springs, north of Salt Lake City.

Twenty-one years later on 27 September 1877, just one month after Young's death, Porter Rockwell and Sylvanus Collett were indicted for the murder of John Aiken. Rockwell was arrested and placed in jail in Salt Lake City, but only for one week. Sick and old, he died nine months later on 8 June 1878. Bill Hickman was living in Fairfield in 1877-78, but he was not similarly indicted for his confessed role in the demise of "Buck" Jones. By this time his involvement had been spelled out in grisly detail in *Brigham's Destroying Angel*. Presumably there was no indictment because there were no witnesses and no body—only Hickman's imaginative account, which was not entirely reliable.

At Collett's four-day trial in October 1878 in Provo's First District Court, witnesses testified according to their religious convictions. Collett claimed he was in Idaho when John Aiken and the three others disappeared. He held to this story despite the testimonies of three witnesses who said they saw him leave Nephi with Rockwell and the four Aiken Gang members. Collett was found not guilty by reason of *"corpus delicti"*—no body had been found. The jury deliberated seven hours. The newspapers and lawyers had predicted his acquittal the day before.

By mid-September 1857, Young had notified Lot Smith, Bill Hickman, Porter Rockwell, and others of his counter-attack plans. A breastwork of dams which could flood the roads were to be built on the west side of Weber and Echo canyons. Fortifications were to be built along the Echo Canyon embankments.

Hickman spent at least part of September in Salt Lake City. On 20 September John Bennion wrote of at least one way Hickman prepared for coming events: "Visited Bro. Hickman and family. He desired [re]baptism. Baptized and confirmed him into the Reformation, blessed his youngest child [seven month-old Laura Isbella, daughter of Sarah Eliza Johnson]".

Hickman was also present at an important meeting at the Social Hall in Salt Lake City on 9 September. A delegation of U.S. officers, including Captain Stewart Van Vliet, assistant quartermaster, had been escorted into the valley to negotiate with Young. After discussing the army's plan to bring U.S. troops into the valley, to which Van Vliet had assumed there would be little resistance, Van Vliet said, "One other item is that of location."

Young replied, "There is a military reserve in Rush Valley," perhaps alluding to Hickman's presence there.

Captain William H. Hooper asked, "What amount of stock could winter in Rush Valley?"

Hickman replied: "Any quantity."

Young then allowed the brethren to question Van Vliet, who admitted he did not think the army trains would reach Great Salt Lake by the fall of 1857.

Van Vliet left the valley with his escort on 16 September and reported from Fort Bridger to Captain Plesanton, adjutant general at Fort Leavenworth:

> During my progress towards Utah I met many people from the Territory, and also several mountain men at Green

River, and all informed me that I would not be allowed to enter Utah, and if I did I would run great risk to losing my life . . . I proceeded alone to Great Salt Lake without molestation—informed Governor B. Young that I desired an interview—appointed the next day . . . 6 days I was treated with hospitality and kindness . . . he talked of persecution of the Mormons, and that the troops now on the march for Utah should not enter the Great Salt Lake Valley . . . [and that they would] resist to the death entrance of troops.

Van Fliet described Young's response to his promise that the army would overrun the ragtag Utah militia:

If you come in strength next year, you will find every house burned to the ground, every tree cut down, and every field laid waste. We have three years provisions on hand, which we will cache, and then take to the mountains and bid defiance to all the powers of government.

I am inclined, however, to believe that the Mormons will not resort to actual hostilities until the last moment.

Their plan of operations will be burn the grass, cut up, the road, stampede the animals, so as to delay the troops until snow commences to fall,—which will render a narrow road to the Valley impassable—last night it commenced to snow at Fort Bridger—a month earlier than usual—I believe troops could force their way in . . .

On 12 September George A. Smith wrote to militia colonel and Mormon stake president in Parowan, Utah, William Dame about Van Vliet's visit and preparations for war:

Dear Pres. Dame, Captain Van Vliet been in the city several days. Bro. Cahoon arrived today, reports pretty well authenticated that about 1000 troops past Laramie. Col. Callisters Regiment camped at Jordan ready to move—400 strong, well equipped and pretty well supplied with ammunition—you may get mighty short notice to march.

All vigilence necessary *to get ammunition,* get guns in order and prepare for winter campaign.

The news of yesterday is that 700 troops have passed Laramie. Their Quartermaster [Van Vliet] returned without contracting for a single article, as he is plainly told the troops will not be allowed to enter this Valley.

Young's proclamation had interrupted supplies headed into the valley, and Hickman wrote of the "great lack of goods and groceries in Salt Lake City that winter." On 9 October, the contractors for Livingston & Kinkaid, a plains freight company, issued the following warning to their drivers: "No supplies are to go by the Army headed for Utah or other points occupied by the Mormons."

Young's inflammatory remarks made in the tabernacle in Salt Lake City on 1 October 1857 reflected the mood of the time:

> I have a right to treat them as a mob, just as though they had been raised and officered in Missouri and sent here expressly to destroy this people. We have been very merciful and lenient to them. As the Lord lives we will waste our enemies by millions, if they send them here to destroy us, and not a man of us will be hurt. That is the method I intend to pursue. Do you want to know what is going to be done with the enemies now on our borders? Men shall be secreted here and there [in the mountains] and shall waste away our enemies, in the name of Israel's God.

On 4 October Daniel Wells, adjutant general of the militia and a counselor to Young, issued the following statement to Joseph Taylor: "On ascertaining the locality or route of the troops, proceed at once to annoy them in every possible way. Use every exertion to stampede their animals and set fire to their trains. Burn the whole country before them and on their flanks. Keep them from sleeping by night surprises . . . God bless you and give you success."

Hickman credited Lot Smith and "his company" with burning three wagon trains, each of which carried five to six thousand pounds of supplies. Others claimed it was Hickman who did the burning. Probably both men carried torches on the evening of 4 October 1857. Only days later, army soldier Eugene Banal reported, "On the east side of Green River we found ironworks of 25 burned wagons—chains, axles, and other wagon parts—covering the trail, on the west side of the Green River, the remains of fifty more wagons."

The next day Hickman began rounding up the scattered government stock which had been abandoned by the soldiers. According to Hickman, he corralled about 275, which he took to Fort Bridger. There he met men from the Utah militia who were bragging about their successes, as well as mountaineers who were running their own stock into the area to keep a close watch on them.

John Bennion, militia leader and Hickman's neighbor in Taylorsville, and his group of fifty-six men and sixty-three horses, arrived to guard Fort Bridger. It was already winter on the Green River plateau, and before the skirmishes would end the men would suffer terribly from the cold.

William Clark, an army teamster, and several other teamsters were captured by Hickman and taken to a spot where Clark says two or three hundred Mormons were camped. He "heard the Mormons pray for over an hour for the destruction of Johnston's Army." According to Clark, the Mormon leaders were all dressed in "buckskin suits covered with beads and fringe, and the finest I had ever seen."

Hickman escorted the captives to Salt Lake City, where they were driven through town as trophies of war. Hickman questioned the teamsters about the army's strength and was pleased to hear they were short on supplies.

Writing on 13 October from his headquarters on the Third Crossing of the Sweetwater to the secretary of war in Washington, D.C., Colonel Johnston complained:

> Tonight two men [arrived] who live at Ft. Laramie and who had been sent on an express to Col. Alexander . . . from them I learn that the Mormons having interposed a force in the rear of our troops, encamped at Ham's Fork of Green River; succeeded in burning 3 supply trains, with their contents . . . [It will be] necessary to protect trains in rear.
>
> Send more men as backup. . . . [W]e will march in the morning, and expect to encamp with Col. Smith tonight. Express says Col. Alexander will attempt to reach Salt Lake City by Bear River . . . much further than the rural routes. Why he selected, I could not learn unless from the probability of the grass being burnt by the Mormons on the direct route. These men say it is certain that they will burn the grass on the route they were about to pursue . . .
>
> The route is beset between this and Ham's Fork with companies of Mormons, so that it is doubtful whether . . . [we] can enter the Valley as planned.

That same day, C. F. Smith, an officer, wrote to the assistant adjutant general at Fort Leavenworth, Kansas:

> Mr. Deshand, my guide, . . . says [he saw] several hundred Mormons, all mounted in the field. They say no more supplies shall go forward; that they will not shed blood, but if

a Mormon is killed by us they will utterly exterminate the gentile army. As to the threats of their leaders to Captain Van Vliet, coupled with the burning of our supply trains—in itself an act of war—is evidence of their treason, I shall regard them as enemies, and fire upon the scoundrels if they give me the least opportunity.

Three days later, Johnston sent a desperate plea to Fort Leavenworth, asking them to "send additional wagons to South Pass and require the men to enlist for 3 months." Johnston assumed command of the U.S. forces on this date. He told Colonel Alexander to "treat as enemies all who oppose your march, molest your trains, appear in arms on your route, or in any manner annoy you."

William Wallace Hammond, a teamster for Russell, Majors, and Waddell, suggested how grim the army's situation was becoming: "The command measures nearly 16 miles when in motion. The weather extremely cold for November. Many of our mules lay down and died . . . nor were we allowed to enter the Salt Lake Valley which some of the men attempted to do, but were brought back to the Fort by scouting parties of cavalry. Over 3,000 men (teamsters) accepted the offer to join the Army at Ft. Bridger—appeared their only salvation."

On 18 October, Johnston sent a dispatch to headquarters from South Pass: "Expect soon to join Col. Alexander at Fontenelle Creek and move down Henry's Fork for the winter. All well, but losing animals from the weather, which is clear and Col. Alexander lost some animals by Mormons. No blood shed."

By 20 October there was a foot of snow at Ham's Fork. A letter from Jesse A. Gove to his wife Maria throws light on the situation the U.S. Army was facing by mid-October.

> Our whole train is 9 miles long it takes 6 companies to guard it. Two Mormon spies were taken in camp yesterday by the 5th Infantry. They are two brothers Hickman, brothers to the celebrated Bill Hickman who is hovering around our rear with a large party. We are in constant expectation of an attack, mostly in the night with a view of stampeding our animals. We sleep on our arms, ready at any moment to fall in to receive our Mormon friends. It snowed yesterday morning and also last night—a Godsend—the grass is wet and they can't burn it.
>
> I do think from all I can learn from the Mt. men, who know them well, that they are the greatest set of villians on

earth. They say that Bill Hickman, who is one of the 70 destroying angels, has murdered more than 100 men in this country with his own hand. We hope to meet him ere long.

Col. Alexander is insane, "an old woman" vacillating conduct—object of ridicule of every officer. He does not know what to do or how to do it . . . says one thing and does another. Twelve days beautiful weather lost.

In contrast Brigham Young was in front of the warm fire in his Salt Lake City office. An express with dispatches to and from the front departed hourly or twice hourly. On 13 October, Young's secretary recorded:

Evening. The President in his office talking with Orson Hyde, and Wilford Woodruff on the probable intentions of the soldiers and the prospects of winning the war. President Young was informed that the cattle still in control of our enemies the soldiers, were guarded by men who had no interest for them and would be glad if our people would drive them off that they might be delivered from the task of minding them, that they might not have to suffer by cold guarding them.

Apparently Bill, in response to a communication from Young, had sent his two brothers to the supply train. It had been learned through previous night-time visits to the supply train that an arms merchant, M. Perry, was willing to sell munitions to the Mormons. "Offer Perry a fair price for his goods," wrote Young, "and advise him to take the Mormon price . . . [or] risk being burned."

George Hickman, the older of the Hickman brothers, was detained by the army until 8 November, when the following letter from Johnston, received by Colonel Waite, counseled: "If there is not sufficient evidence against Mr. George W. Hickman, now a prisoner in your charge, to convict him of being a spy, or to make him amenable to the civil authority, . . . that he be released from confinement, his mule restored to him, and he be sent immediately from camp."

Meanwhile, Bill Hickman's group had not been idle. On Friday, 16 October, Alexander sent an express to Young to report that seven hundred head of cattle had been driven off. According to Hickman: "We kept watch of the U.S. camps every day, and if a party attempted to leave we would make a rush for them and run them into camp again. One day we moved up the creek about 4 miles, and we saw a vacancy between them and their cattle. We made a rush and drove off seven hundred and fifty head, taking all the fat cattle they had, and some mules. Horses and mules were taken several times after this."

Hickman was at the same time dealing with another munitions trader, or sutler, on the Green River. Richard Yates, like M. Perry, was playing both sides for the best price. Yates had several kegs of powder for sale, a quantity of lead and caps, and other supplies worth several hundred dollars. He refused to sell his goods to the Mormons unless they agreed to buy all of his supplies. When Yates decided to sell to the U.S. regulars, army captain Albert Tracy wrote in his journal that Yates "disappeared . . . went up the pocket of the Lord."

The news regarding Yates had made him suspect as a spy, and he was arrested and marched to jail at Fort Bridger, probably on 14 October. Yates was then turned over to the custody of Bill Hickman. The army had his brother George, and now Hickman had Yates.

Hickman had his prisoner shackled with a common trace-chain on his ankle. According to Hickman, Yates was carrying a "fine gold watch and nine hundred dollars in gold, all in twenty-dollar gold pieces." Hickman claimed that Yates gave him the items "to carry."

Early on 18 October they set out on horseback from Fort Bridger for Salt Lake City. Half way down Echo Canyon at the headquarters of Daniel Wells, Hickman delivered some letters and asked Wells what to do with his prisoner. According to Hickman, Wells said, "He ought to be killed; but take him on; you will probably get an order when you get to Col. N. V. Jones's camp," which was twelve miles west.

Four miles short of Jones's camp, Hickman met Joseph A. Young, who was on his way to Wells's camp with dispatches from his father. It was during this chance meeting that Hickman later claimed he was told Brigham Young "wanted Yates killed." Joseph Young had left his father on Sunday, 18 October, at 8:56 a.m., accompanied by his brother John Young and William Kimball. All, including Brigham Young and Hosea Stout, were later indicted by a grand jury investigating the murder.

Yates was apparently not murdered on the spot but was accosted after dark at Jones's camp, a mile below the mouth of

Echo Canyon. According to Hickman, Hosea Stout and another man asked "if Yates was asleep." "I told them he was," wrote Hickman, "upon which his brains were knocked out with an axe." Picks and spades were brought, and a grave three feet deep was dug by the campfire, "all hands assisting."

Dan Jones operated the next camp about ten or twelve miles down the canyon. Hickman and his two companions, Meacham and Flack, arrived there in the early morning hours. Thomas Hickman had been sent on the night before, probably to prevent his being connected with Yates's killing. "They seemed almost frozen," Lorenzo Brown, who was at the camp, noted in his diary. "Hickman asked me if I had any whiskey. I told him I had not. He then asked if I had coffee. I replied that we had."

While the coffee was brewing, Hickman confessed to Jones that Yates had been killed and buried. The four men then rode to the next station even though they had already spent twenty-four hours on the trail without resting. Jones's account of these events was published in 1890—nineteen years after Hickman's testimony before the grand jury and over thirty after the event. According to Jones, "Brigham Young would not have ordered such a killing, and that Bill Hickman did it for Yates' money." By 1890 this was the preferred story.

Hickman's group arrived in Salt Lake City after dark on 20 October. According to Hickman, he went to see Brigham Young with Yates's $900. Young's office journal records no visit from Hickman or his associate Flack.

Young's office journal recorded William Kimball's return on Wednesday, 21 October, with the news that "the army is not coming, but settling in for the winter." On Thursday, Young left his office for the first time since the crisis had begun and went to spend time on his farm. Until the spring thaw, he would not have to worry about an invasion.

The severe winter was one Wyoming pioneers would recall for years. By the end of October or early November, Colonel Johnston reported:

> There is no fuel but the wild sage and willow, and there is little pasture for the half frozen cattle. Our march commenced on the sixth of November, and on the previous night 500 of our strongest cattle were taken by the Mormons. We have 2600 men wintering in a region of 7000 ft. where at night the temperature is always below zero—we

have 3150 bedticks and 723 blankets... some of the men are already barefooted and others have no covering for feet but moccasins. We have one wagon entirely freighted with camp kettles; with nothing to cook, and no salt with which to season their nothingness.

The camp on Black's Fork, thirty miles east of Fort Bridger, was labeled the "Camp of Death." Five hundred animals perished around the camp the night of 6 November. Fifteen oxen were found huddled together in one heap, "frozen stiff."

The army moved slowly westward, taking thirty days to advance the final thirty-five miles to Fort Bridger. There they found the fort burned. The army began construction of Camp Scott, two miles to the east, where they would spend the rest of the winter, "sitting in the snow eating 3 crackers a day." When the Mormons learned of the troops' plight, they were dispersed and spent the winter at home. Alfred Cumming, newly appointed governor of the Utah territory, wrote the following epistle to the "People of the Utah Territory" on 21 November from Camp Scott:

> On 11th of July, 1857, the President appointed me to preside over the executive department of the government of this Territory. I arrived the 19th of this month. —I will proceed to make the preliminary arrangements for the temporary organization of the territorial government . . . many treasonable acts of violence having recently been committed by lawless individuals, supposed to have been commanded by the late executive. *Such persons are in a state of rebellion.* Proceedings will be instituted against them in a court organized by Chief Justice Eckles.

All winter the pressure was on for the Mormons to surrender and to allow the army to enter the valley. In December 1857, a bill of indictment was issued by the grand jury of the District Court of Salt Lake City, convened at Camp Scott, charging Brigham Young, Heber Kimball, Daniel Wells, John Taylor, George D. Grant, Lot Smith, Porter Rockwell, William A. Hickman, Albert Carrington, Joseph Taylor, William Stowell, Lewis Robison, Joshua Terry, John Harvey, Daniel Jones, Phineas Young, William Young, Robert Burton, James Ferguson, and Ephraim Hanks with treason against the United States.

By January 1858, Bill Hickman had returned to Taylorsville, but the army was only three days' march away and no settlement had been reached. In the spring Mormons were asked to sign the "Mormon War Conveyances," legal documents which transferred all property to Brigham Young. As absolute owner and controller of all Mormon property, Young's hand would be strengthened in his negotiations with federal authorities.

A major breakthrough occurred on 6 April 1858 when President Buchanan, at the recommendation of Thomas L. Kane, offered "to the inhabitants of Utah, *who shall submit to the laws, a free pardon for the sedition and treasons heretofore by them committed.*" Not learning of Buchanan's proclamation until June, Brigham Young continued to negotiate troop movement through Salt Lake City and decided that the Saints should leave the valley. He advised the Mormons: "We do not want you to burn down your houses, but leave them in the care of those that are going to stay."

On 26 March, John Bennion and Bill Hickman went to see the First Presidency to discuss where the West Jordan Ward should move. They were assigned to settle in Pond Town (Salem) and Spanish Fork. They were to take furniture and supplies and leave wood at the house doors to ignite in case the army tried to occupy the city rather than march through to Rush Valley. Bill Hickman was appointed to supervise the resettlement of his ward and was made a member of the ward bishopric. He was released three months later.

On 8 June Governor Cumming and his wife, Elizabeth, officially arrived in Salt Lake City. (They had been unofficially living in the city since March.) Two days later, Brigham Young, Heber Kimball, Daniel Wells, the twelve apostles, and twenty to thirty bishops, high priests, and elders rode into the city to greet the army officers. Young's mansion was opened and a banquet prepared.

Ten days later, 200 to 300 Mormon refugees who had evacuated the city and were camped at Utah Lake were given permission by Brigham Young to return to their homes. They arrived in time to see the army march into the valley. Flags throughout the city were flown at half-mast. The troops marched to Twenty-first South, where they turned west to the Jordan River and made camp on what is today Redwood Road. They reached Fairfield on 6 July.

Hickman assessed his own postwar situation: "Prejudice existed against me in the United States Army, because of the course I had taken." And because the U.S. Army was the apparent victor, Hickman could not anticipate a very comfortable future in Utah.

– 10 –

The Dust Settles

In November 1858, Brigham Young recorded in his journal: "Bill Hickman had his horse stolen in the street last night, with saddle. A few hours before it was stolen, he was offered five hundred dollars for it. Thieves are getting a stronghold in Salt Lake City, stealing horses in the streets through the day and wagons out of yards at night." The *Valley Tan*, a weekly Gentile newspaper printed from 6 November 1858 to 29 February 1869, confirmed Young's comments about an abundance of horse thieves: "This City and vicinity have suffered to a considerable extent within the past two weeks from the depredations of those who deal in stock without paying for them. Several persons have had their horses taken in broad daylight."

In late 1858 and early 1859, the *Deseret News* recorded numerous incidents of cattle and horse stealing between Camp Floyd and Orem. According to Hickman, he tried to persuade those he was acquainted with to "quit and behave themselves." Some told him to mind his business. Late in the year army engineers opened up a new and better road between Camp Floyd and Fort Bridger, one of the benefits of the army's stay in the valley. But this road also gave thieves a better escape route to the east.

On 4 August 1858, General Johnston sent a communique to Colonel William Hoffman at Fort Bridger in which he blamed the missing cattle from his army stock in Rush Valley on Indians. Three months later the following editorial appeared in the *Valley Tan*: "The city and vicinity is infested with a set of horse thieves which are supposed to be regularly organized. Let everyone look to their stables and corrals."

Who were these thieves? The war had brought not only U.S. soldiers into Utah but also hundreds of camp followers. Much of the blame for the mounting crime could be attributed to such undesirables living near Camp Floyd—but not all. During 1858-59, at least two local gangs of horse thieves were operating in Utah: Bill Hickman's and that of Joachim "Cub" Johnson.

In defense of Camp Floyd, *Valley Tan* editor Kirk Anderson insisted on 6 November 1858 that "drunkenness and rowdyism" were not evident at the camp. "On the contrary the most strict discipline and rigid rules have been enforced." The *Valley Tan* later noted that "Hickman and Burnham have 900 head of cattle, all in fine condition destined for sale in California."

During this time Hickman was serving Brigham Young as one of his spies. Young needed informers to watch the army and to contact prominent Gentiles about their views of the church and chose Hickman. On 21 December 1858, Young recorded in his journal:

> William A. Hickman called on President Brigham Young, and told him he had had a private conversation with Judge St. Clair, the judge remarked to him that the Mormons were unwilling to admit that they were guilty of treason or any other charge with which they had been tried, but before he was through with them, he would show them that they had done a great deal. He said he had seen some Mormons that he liked but the leading men and the public generally he despised and will make them know he was after them.

Hickman wrote about his favorable relationship with Chief Justice D. R. Eckles, "a fine clever old gentleman" with whom he spent "many a social evening." That July Hickman took his colleague, Hosea Stout, to meet Eckles. Later Hickman would remind Brigham Young that this friendship was carried on mostly to discover what was going on at Camp Floyd and among the Gentiles:

> I had an object in view in keeping the company which I have, it seemed to open without exertion so that I could find out everything that was going on in town at Camp Floyd, Judge Eckles holding back nothing, this all came about with having saying ought against you or the Church. Their feelings and some several items I had learned, thought would be a benefit.

Brigham Young was painfully aware of the army's presence on the valley's west side, and although he relied on men like

Hickman and Rockwell to keep him informed, his journal comment of 22 April 1859 shows he may have harbored some suspicions about them: "It is rumored that five Marshals left Camp Floyd yesterday sworn to arrest or kill Bill Hickman on the spot. Bill *was warned and left home in time.*" The order to send U.S. marshals had been issued two weeks earlier, on 6 April, in a letter from General Johnston to Captain H. R. Selden: "The Deputy Marshal of the Territory of Utah will make a requisition upon you for 30 men, rank and file to serve as a posse in the arrest of certain persons in San Pete Valley—bring the prisoners to camp under guard."

Considering Hickman's status under the new territorial government, he was able to maintain a surprisingly normal life during the summer of 1859, even marrying his tenth wife, an orphan named Mary Jane Hetherington. Hickman was forty-four years old. Mary Jane Hetherington was nineteen. Her parents, non-Mormons emigrating to California, had died in Iowa and Nebraska. Mary Jane had ridden with a Mormon wagon train to Ogden, where she converted to Mormonism. She married Hickman on 2 June 1859 in the Salt Lake Endowment House with Brigham Young officiating.

In early July 1859, Josiah Arnold of the West Jordan Ward was excommunicated for apostasy. Arnold and a man named C. M. Drown were found murdered a few weeks later. Hickman was charged. Hickman wrote about Drown in his autobiography: "His common character was not good," citing horse and cattle stealing as his primary faults. Drown had apparently stolen a widow's horse—though he eventually repaid her.

Judge Cradlebaugh, a federal appointee, blamed Hickman's mistrust of Arnold and Drown on their conversion to spiritualism. Cradlebaugh also claimed a promissory note in the amount of $480 had been brought to his court by Drown, who had sued Hickman for non-payment. Cradlebaugh had ruled in Drown's favor. This version is confirmed by T. B. H. Stenhouse, though he may have relied on Cradlebaugh.

According to Hickman, Drown's name came up in conversation with Brigham Young, who said he should be "used up" or killed. But Hickman said he was welcoming the editor of a new newspaper, the *Mountaineer*, at the time of the shooting. Drown and Arnold were in a Salt Lake City house a few blocks away when they were shot. According to Cradlebaugh, they were in the "midst of a seance" when first Drown then Arnold were gunned down. Arnold was shot while trying to escape.

Hickman was indicted for Drown's murder in early August 1859. In his memoirs, Hickman claimed a man named "Matthews" confessed to him that he and two accomplices had kicked in the door of Drown's house and shot Drown and Arnold. A Mr. Blair, Hickman's attorney, entered the motion for a new trial on 12 August 1859.

In the evening of 29 August, Daniel Wells, Albert Carrington, and George A. Smith met with Brigham Young. The conversation concerned "the reckless manner in which the assassins of C. M. Drown [there is no mention of Arnold], had fired—indiscriminately among the people in the houses." The next day, in third judicial court, both sides agreed to a trial without jury. Less than three weeks later, an indictment for the murder of C. M. Drown was issued against Rodney D. Swazey, apparently one of Matthews's two companions. No motive was given.

Still rumor of Hickman's involvement persisted. In 1868, Hickman complained in a bitter letter to Young that he was tired of being accused of murders he had never committed.

According to *Brigham's Destroying Angel,* Hickman was involved in yet another controversy that year when a California man named Batey or Beatty was shot south of Ogden in a private feud with a man named "Cub" Johnson. Hickman was accused of the murder but claimed innocence. According to Hickman, "Cub" Johnson was arraigned for Beatty's murder in Farmington, Utah.

During this period, Hickman's neighbor, John Bennion, was beginning to feel less friendly toward him:

> Sunday, October 23, 1859: Attended a meeting of the high priests in the ward—the first since our return home from the south. Meeting in the school house. B[isho]p. Gardner presiding. He spoke at considerable length and with freedom rebuking sin and encouraging those that do well, after the meeting I and Samuel [his brother], had a long talk. I reported to him and the Bishop some things concerning W. A. Hickman and family which conduct was unchristian like.

From October to mid-December, Bennion's diary records several meetings with the Hickman family. There is no indication that Hickman himself was present on any of the five occasions mentioned. In fact, the nature of the visits suggests that Hickman was not at home. His family was praying for his safety. Another of Hickman's neighbors reported that Hickman was "in hiding most of the year."

– 11 –

The "Hickman Hounds" and the Shootout

Bill Hickman's gang was labeled the "Hickman Hounds" by Brigham Young. There were probably no more than fifteen or twenty active gang members at any given time and membership often changed. The twenty-three known members were George W. Hickman, Thomas Jefferson Hickman, and James Barton Hickman—all brothers; Samuel Meacham, Jason Luce, Wilford Luce, and John M. Luce—all brothers-in-law; Samuel Monroe Butcher, a son-in-law; Emory Meacham, a son-in-law and a brother-in-law; and John Flack, Dick Wheeler, John Wakeley, Bill Woodland, Charles Harrison, Isaac Neibaur, Moroni Clauson, Wood Reynolds, John P. Smith, George Heath, James Rhodes, Louis Dauganser, Lott Huntington, and Thomas J. Wheeler.

In 1879, Hickman's nephew, Warren E. Hickman, published a thinly fictionalized account of his uncle's career, which claimed that Hickman led a large gang whose activities spread from "Utah to eastern Colorado, with links to central Kansas gangs." He describes Hickman as "a hard, reckless, daring spirit, who at 18 years of age crossed the plains with Brigham Young . . . and became the famous 'Danite Chief,' the military leader of the Mormon Church." (In reality, Hickman had joined the Mormon church at age twenty-one and was thirty-four when he crossed the plains.)

No other source hints that Hickman's activities extended into central Colorado and Kansas. But he may have traveled there when U.S. marshals were pursuing him. He was evidently absent from Taylorsville from September 1859 until Christmas. According to Warren's book, the Hickman brothers were at the Colorado gold diggings when their youngest brother, Martin, was killed by a claim-jumper. The next day, the story continues, two of the brothers found the guilty man and "did him in the same." Warren claims that the brothers "all took a leading part in the development of Colorado, with one brother still living in Bent County, in 1879." Thomas Jefferson Hickman moved to Bent County after leaving Utah in 1869. In 1877 he was appointed county sheriff, his earlier wild days mostly forgotten.

How many Hickmans were present at the Pike's Peak gold rush in 1859, or contributed significantly to the development of Colorado, is unknown. Warren Hickman's story shows them to be rough, short-tempered, trigger-happy fortune hunters. Wherever Bill Hickman was in 1859, he was back in Salt Lake City by Christmas, when he was shot by Lott Huntington and almost killed.

According to Hickman's autobiography, the shooting was a consequence of his attempts to curb the horse-stealing that was rampant in the area. He tried his best to stop the rustling by talking to those involved, "even threatening to get them if they did not stop." According to Hickman, Porter Rockwell went after one group of thieves who had taken horses from a government freighter and brought them back to Salt Lake City.

Later seven of the men Rockwell had caught found Hickman on the edge of town and threatened to shoot him. But Bill was able to jerk a revolver out from each side of his belt and chase them away. He thought the matter forgotten, even though he heard threats against him for several more weeks.

However, the seven men soon took seventeen horses from Mr. Gerrish of the mercantile firm of Gilbert and Gerrish, both friends of Hickman. The merchants asked Hickman to help them recover their horses. After contacting Joe Rhodes, a member of "Cub" Johnson's gang, and offering him $100 to tell him where the horses were, Hickman learned that they had been taken to Cedar County. As a result of this disclosure, Thomas J. Wheeler, another member of Johnson's gang, was arrested. Furious, Johnson's gang came looking for Hickman at the home of his son-in-law, Samuel Monroe Butcher. The following Sunday afternoon, after a heated exchange of oaths, Hickman daring them to shoot, the rival gang members shot it out just outside the Townsend Hotel on First South and West Temple. In his diary, George Laub wrote of "two parties of rude persons coming in collusion with each other."

Seven contemporary diary accounts agree on most details of the fight. Hickman was shot by Lott Huntington; no one expected him to survive. Lorenzo Brown wrote:

> December 25, 1859. Coming from meeting I heard the report of 30-40 pistol shots fired in rapid succession in the space of 5-10 minutes. William A. Hickman and Lot Huntington were both wounded in the thigh. The first is considered dangerous. The shot struck his watch and glanced down and lodged against the bone in 2 pieces. One of the pieces has been extracted and a piece of thigh bone. Several splinters or bone are sticking in the flesh. Huntington's is not serious but the ball is not extracted. They are both desperate characters and are reputed horse thieves of some notoriety and have gathered each a little band about them from different settlements—so says rumor.

Brigham Young wrote: "December 26, 1859. About 1:00 p.m. yesterday, a disgraceful affair occurred on Main Street near the Townsend Hotel. A difficulty between Wm. A. Hickman and Lott Huntington over the division of some stolen property. Hickman and his party retired to Hickman's son-in-law, and a physician was sent for."

That same day, Apostle Amasa Lyman thundered from the pulpit, pointing a finger to the West Jordan area:

> The spirit of thieving stalks the land—gets hold of unguarded youth, causes them to steal from neighbors. Don't let your sons be corrupted—know where they are—Many deceive, not just Bill Hickman and his gang. Sons go into the streets of the city only to hear that stealing from Gentiles is "OK," and are told that the President of the Church says so—all lies to lead the unwary from the truth.

A few days later, Hickman, lying in excruciating pain at his daughter Katharine Butcher's house, wrote to Brigham Young:

I am glad I am able to sit up in bed and write you—my very soul is grieved with regard to misrepresentations that have reached you. When my Bro. [George] told me what you said, made the cold sweat run off me and I almost sank under it. Hear me and then say where I am wrong. Some ten days previous to my being shot, I was at John Wakeley's taking breakfast. John was not at home, his family and Bill Woodland were there. "Cub" Johnson, Lott Huntington and about 8 others came, said I was hard man to find, said they had some business with me invited me out, we stood but a few steps from the door—he accused me of being round his house to kill him, which I denied, then he accused John Flack, Jason Luce, *and all the boys that live with* [me], which I told him was false. About this time Lott came up swore it was so, and would kill me.

Upon this the crowd gathered round. Most of them hands on their pistols, and I thought I had to go up—I told them to turn themselves loose for they should never have a better chance, and if fight was what was wanted I was ready and willing a man as they ever saw. This put a check to things and they calmed considerable. I then demanded their author, they said they would give none, but said they would some other time. Next, they accused me in being officious[?], in having Port Rockwell go south after them and Johnson-this they said they believed, and if they knew it was so they would shot me—I told them I knew nothing about their animals nor Port going after them.

Then they turned themselves loose in general terms, Cub and Lott, swearing and saying did not care a d--- for god almighty, General Johnson [sic] or old Brigham. Says they, Bill Hickman, if Brigham was to try to stop us in another expedition we would go up and cut his throat like a dog. They were going to do as they pleased, and I nor no other person must be in their way—I talked till they calmed and left—this was the first I knew they had anything against me—all their accusations against me were false, no foundation for one word.

Some four of the boys and myself came in town on Friday previous to Christmas taking a sleigh ride. I cautioned them to keep strait [sic] which they did.

The same knight [sic], I was sitting by the fire at Butcher's, my son-law,—my daughter says, "look out," and the blanket was shoved aside from the window and pistol polked [sic] through at me—when she spoke he ran, but did not go far and as their [sic] was no stir after, remaining about

15 minutes he Lott in company with a man I did not know, came and raped [sic] at the door. Came in very friendly. Now, he was not out of site [sic], from the time he poked his pistol in the window' at me, till he came in. Next evening he came again. With some 3 or four, my boys were all with me—he asked if I had anything against him. I told him nothing—only the way he treated me at Wakeley's. He admitted he should not have done so, so this ended the matter.

We started up town. On the way he says to me, "When you find out who has told all these stories on you, you will find it to be Dick Wheeler." Next day I seen Dick and asked him. He said he never said a word against me in his life—On Sunday, Christmas, I was in the alley at Townsends—had sent for the sleigh to go home. All hands sober. I care anything being drunk that day. Wheeler was there. Lott came up, this being the first I had seen of him that day. . . . With the bitterest kind of any oath, [he] drew his pistol cocked, which I caught—I thought first I would kill him. Drew my knife with the other hand but, he[l]d up after starting a blow. All hands says to me, "Don't kill him." I stopped, someone steped [sic] in between us. He fell back a few feet and shot me.

I drew my pistol, but before I got it out of the scabbord he shot at me again—as I brought my pistol on him, he wheeled to run. I shot. He jumped some 3 feet high, clapping his hand behind him. He then run out from the alley about 50 steps, wheeled, shot twice at J. Luce, then at John Flack, upon which the boys returned the compliments. Butcher says he shot at him also, but this I did not see. I shot 4 times. Followed him to George Grants—Now Br. Brigham this is true as I know how to tell it,—one thing more, the party at Wakeley's swore vengence [sic] on Port Rockwell. Ron Clauson says "Boys don't bother yourselves about him. I intend to get him."

The original of this letter, written less than one week after the shooting, agrees with a version printed in *Brigham's Destroying Angel.*

Young replied to Hickman's letter in early January 1860, but his letter has been lost. Hickman wrote again before 19 January, and this letter gives a good sense of Young's concerns about Hickman:

Dear Bro Brigham,

With regards to my associates and drinking. I had an object in view in keeping the company which I have. It seemed to open without exertion, so that I could find out everything that was going on in town at Camp Floyd, Judge Ecles [Eckles], holding back nothing. This all came about with having saying [said] ought against you or the Church. Their feelings and some several items I had learned. Thought [it] would be a benefit and on Saturday before Christmas I came up to communicate with you. Waited an hour, but you did not come in. Now, the more whiskey they would drink the freer they would talk, and of course I had to keep up my corners. I did so with them when we had no conversation in order to keep natural—I have seen that I was watched. I knew it. I supposed your ears were filled with stories against me, but I was determined to [tell] no person till I did you. I have had the question asked, "Bill, what's going on?" My reply would be, "O nothing, but drinking whiski [sic]," now in these associations I thought I was doing rite [sic] I thought if I could find out anything that would benefit you I [line missing].

I know I have drank a great deal of whisky, but it is no object for me to quit. If you say it is best, I will never taste another drop. If you say leave my Gentile associations, I am willing. I'm sure it is no pleasure to me. No person has seen me drunk in the streets, notwithstanding all my whiskeying. No person has seen one of the boys drunk that live with (me), drunk in town. I lecture them at home with my family once a week. We attend our prayers regular. Notwithstanding my reported wickedness. This you can learn from the teachers of our ward or our neighbors—our aim and intentions is to do right and I have faults and imperfections and do wrong, but when ever I know it, I repent as fast as I can—I may have many faults that I do not know of—Bro. Brigham please forgive me of what I have done wrong. I know this is the work of the almighty. I know who you are. It has long since been shown to me, long since. I delight in the Latterday work. I hope whether I live or die whether I obtain [line missing].

I know I have been profane but I scarse [sic] ever use the name of God. When I am very mad I check myself I do not guard against it as I keep trying to overcome it—.

There are many other things I would like to say but I am tired. I have been 3 days writing—it may sound flat but it [is] the best I can do in my feeble state.

May the lord bless, perserve and prosper you is my prayer all the day long.

Wm. A. Hickman

Two Mormon doctors attended Hickman after the shooting, probing for the bullet and bone fragments in his thigh. They reported him mortally wounded and left. Other physicians called were dismissed. Hickman's thigh swelled and was kept in ice packs for three weeks. Dr. Hobbs of the U. S. Army, a cousin of Bernetta, visited from Camp Floyd with a board of physicians. Hobbs and his associates "re-opened the dangerously infected wound and extracted a dirty green piece of cotton saturated with something—which the first doctors had failed to remove."

In spite of his precarious hold on life, threats from the other gang continued. On 19 January 1860, a drunken Joe Rhodes, no doubt afraid Hickman would reveal his duplicity to other Johnson gang members, attempted to enter Hickman's room with two revolvers. Jason Luce, posted as a guard, ran him through with his bowie knife—eleven times. Charles Walker mentioned the incident in his diary entry for 20 January, 1860: "It seems last night sometime that a man named Joe Rhodes was stabbed in a shocking manner and died very soon after by one Jason Luce who did it in self Defence. I think if they would drink less whisky and work for their living they would be better off than killing one another." Luce was tried in court and acquitted. Three years later he would be executed for another murder committed in self defense.

Hickman required crutches for six months, and the effects of the shooting plagued him throughout the remainder of his life. Four times he almost died from the metal and shattered bone that remained in his thigh. For the remaining twenty-four years of his life he exhibited a "shuffling gait." Hickman's wife Minerva gave birth to a son on 22 May 1860 and named him Survivor in memory of the traumatic event. The name was passed on for three generations among Minerva's descendants.

– 12 –

The Beating of Governor Dawson

As Bill Hickman remembered it, "Nothing uncommon transpired in '60-61." There were a few murders, some "for stealing and some for seduction," but "some of the greatest scoundrels ran untouched."

Actually, 1860 began badly for Hickman. On Sunday, 5 January, only ten days after the shooting incident, the bishop of his Mormon congregation spoke "forcibly on the workers of iniquity," promising that he "would do his duty in those things." Lying near death in his daughter's house, Hickman received word that he had been disfellowshipped. His neighbor John Bennion chronicled in his journal that fall his own discussions with the bishop about Hickman. Bennion wanted Hickman excommunicated—a more severe church action than disfellowshipment. On 26 August, Bennion wrote:

> I spoke privately with [the bishop] about W. A. Hickman. At our evening meeting the matter was further presented. The Bishop, counsel, and Elder Heywood were present. Bishop Gardner said there was much prejudice against W. A. Hickman and that he knew nothing against him, as nothing had been reported to him officially. He intimated that W. A. Hickman was apologetic and that he would stand by him or any other Brother until he knew of their guilt. Hickman being called upon confessed to his weaknesses and foibles like other men, but strongly denied his guilt as to things commonly reported on him, stealing etc. Bishop Gardner

requested any who knew anything against Hickman to report to him and to stop running to Bishop Hunter or he would be after them with a sharpstick. Meeting closed.

In October Bennion was still concerned about the matter of Bill Hickman's church status:

> Saturday, October 13, 1860: Went to the city met Bishop Gardner, had a talk with him about W. A. Hickman's wicked course for sometime past. He said that up until now he had been bound and could not act, I told him I was not bound, neither was I afraid to oppose the wickedness of any man, that it was my duty to expose. We got home about sundown. In the evening I met with the Bishop and his counselors and parties concerned with trying George Hickman for stealing mules. When about to commence the trial, Elder Hyde came in and by Bishop Gardner's solicitation he preached and *the trial was postponed.*
>
> After meeting the Bishop, the counsel, and Elder Hyde had a long talk in my house. Bro. Hyde said, speaking of stealing that a man may steal and be influenced by the spirit of the Lord to do it, that Hickman had done it in years past. Said that he never would institute a trial against a brother for stealing from the Gentiles, but stealing from his brother, he was down on it. He laid down much teaching on the subject.

Orson Hyde, a member of the Council of Twelve Apostles, was an important Hickman defender. Hickman had saved his life in 1849, and he could not bring himself to condemn Hickman yet. As late as 1872, Hickman would use Hyde's line of reasoning in his own defence: he could not understand why people chastised him when all he did was to steal from the Gentiles.

Bennion attended yet another meeting on the matter of Hickman's church status the next day: "Sunday October 14, 1860: Went to meeting at the mill to hear Bro. Hyde . . . he gave much good instruction, spoke on last night's intention to try Hickman—give it as the word of the Lord to set him free for the past, bid him go and sin no more." Two months later, Elder Heber C. Kimball contradicted Hyde in public: "Certain ones say that we justify stealing from unbelievers but we do not and they who say so shall be cursed, they shall be poor and vagabounds [sic] on the earth, and all the people said, 'Amen.'" Kimball's statement underscored the changing times, the isolated frontier giving way to political considerations. The U.S. Army was no longer simply the enemy. A greater accommodation to the occupying forces was emerging.

Also, Hickman's unorthodox way of earning a living was being threatened by his continuing precarious health. In January three suits were brought against him by Bradford Leonard in the probate court of Elias Smith. Leonard wanted outstanding debts reconciled before Hickman died. The first suit was a claim for $237 against Hickman, Charles Harrison, and John Wakely. Leonard won by default. An appeal was filed three months later. Again Hickman lost. Leonard also made a claim of $395.83 against Hickman and S. M. Johnson—again the judgment was granted to Leonard by default. The third judgment was a demand for $108, which in May 1960 Judge Smith also ruled as "Judgment by default."

That spring, on 6 April, Hickman borrowed $129.25 from Brigham Young. He would ask Young for money two additional times in the next few years, in October of 1861 and again in July 1868. The second loan followed an incident which only complicated Hickman's health problems. In the fall of 1861 Hickman was just beginning to walk, though with a pronounced limp, when he was shot again—this time by himself. John Bennion described the accident in his journal: "Last evening, Saturday, September 21, 1861, Hickman was shot by his own pistol (accidentally) wound dangerous as he was waiting for the threshing machine." Later daughter Minerva Lerona would recall the incident, which took place when she was only five years old: "Something caught his pistol. It fell to the ground and went off and shot him thru the liver. 'I am shot,' he cried as he ran to gramma Bernetta. He prayed, asked God to spare him, and he lived 30 more years." He would actually live only twenty-two more years. Hickman did not include this embarrassing event in his memoirs.

Three weeks after the accidental shooting he penned the following letter to Brigham Young on the matter of the second loan:

> Sir, I am sorry to have troubled you for a loan, but it seemed to be the only chance. If I had been able to get around I could have got it. I have some money due me which I will get soon as I am able to be about and pay you. I am truly thankful for your kindness in letting me have the money and hope it will

not be many day[s] until I shall be able to see you, which I am very anxious to do. May the Lord bless and preserve you to carry on his great work.

This letter to Young does not begin to explain the precarious situation in which the large and growing Hickman clan languished. Five children were born to Hickman in 1861-62. Six more followed in 1864-65. All eleven entered a household without a consistent means of support. Minerva Lenora gives an idea of the circumstances in a letter she wrote shortly before her death: "My father's women were industrious. They used to spin and knit. By 11 years old I could spin three skanes of yarn a day and knit a sock a day. We got a $1.00 a piece for our socks and 75 cents for mittens." Minerva Lenora was one of Hickman's children who never received formal schooling.

Perhaps poverty was one of the reasons Hickman's fifth wife, Hannah Dyantha Horr, left him to marry Hyrum Elliott Byington on 18 February 1861. Her sister Mary, Hickman's ninth wife, would also later move in with Byington, to whom she was sealed by proxy on 9 December 1896. Both sisters had two children by Hickman whom they raised under the name Byington.

Hickman did manage to build a house for his family during this period. Ironically it was the departing federal army which provided a windfall for Hickman and other settlers beginning in the fall of 1860. The Civil War seemed remote from Utah, but it had one favorable effect on Salt Lake Valley residents. During the summer of 1860, word came to Colonel Cooke, the commander at Camp Floyd, that the troops were needed back in the states or along the Oregon Trail, protecting immigrants. Within weeks, three companies of dragoons moved to Fort Hall in Idaho. Camp Floyd would be closed as soon as possible. This announcement was met with considerable rejoicing.

Soon Fairfield, Utah, the site of Camp Floyd, would be returned to the sleepy community it was before the U.S. Army arrived in 1858. Because of the proximity of the army, Fairfield had become the third largest town in Utah, and probably the wildest. At its height there were 4,000 soldiers, 40,000 oxen and 1,000 mules in the vicinity. Camp followers, including liquor merchants, prostitutes, and others, added to the riotous atmosphere. The *Deseret News* reported on 21 April 1860 that in "Fairfield in the past few months it was exceedingly rare to find virtue in either men or women."

THE BEATING OF GOVERNOR DAWSON

The army began to sell off government stores at Camp Floyd during the summer of 1860. Prices were ridiculously low. Approximately four million dollars worth of goods were sold for $100,000. Only ammunition stores were kept off the market and destroyed, presumably to keep them from the treasonous Mormons. Flour sold for 50 cents per 100 pound sack, bacon for one-fourth cent per pound. There was lumber for the taking. The sale of condemned or badly damaged goods continued through the fall of 1860 and into the following summer, with a final sale in August 1861. This final sale was an economic bonanza to locals that provided the base for several local fortunes.

According to Hickman, he bought ten wagon loads of goods. What he purchased or how he used the goods, he does not say. But his daughter, Minerva Lerona, born in 1856, reported in a letter: "Pa bought a small piece of land below our old place by John Bennions, built a big log house with upstairs in it—we lived there two years while he went to Bingham Canyon to work in the mines." Minerva mentions that Hickman's brother James "came from the east and lived with them one winter before he moved to Bingham Canyon and the mines." Ten wagon loads of building materials could have provided lumber, doors, and windows for a two-storey house. Brigham Young's Forest Farm home was built with a purchase of fifty wagon loads of Camp Floyd materials.

Hickman augmented his income by joining his brother at the mines and by getting back to some practice of law in the spring of 1861. He also served as guide for the expedition of Colonel Davies, newly appointed superintendent of Indian Affairs for Utah, to the Goshutes and Shoshones in Ruby Valley, Idaho.

By late 1861 Hickman's name was once again publicly associated with troubles related to the actions of members of his gang. Governor Alfred Cumming had left Utah in the spring of 1860, after serving two years—an event Hickman chronicled in his autobiography. Cumming was replaced in the fall of 1861 by John M. Dawson, who served as Utah's governor for only twenty-one days before being driven from the territory. On his way out, as he passed Ephraim Hank's station between Big Mountain and Little Mountain on the road to Fort Bridger, he was attacked by several members of Hickman's gang. The popular story in Salt Lake City was that Dawson was assaulted because he had spoken "seductive language to a woman in the city." Dawson was nearly beaten to death and died from head injuries a few months later. The beating occurred the night of 31 December 1861.

Hickman wrote in some detail about this incident in his autobiography. The substance of his account is confirmed by the probate court action filed before Judge E. Smith on 13 January 1862. The indictment named Wood Reynolds, Jason Luce, John M. Luce, Isaac Neibaur, Wilford Luce, and Moroni Clawson, all members of Hickman's gang, and a new addition, Lott Huntington, formerly of Cub Johnson's gang. Hickman and Huntington had apparently reconciled since the time Huntington shot Bill in the hip.

The seven men involved in the beating of Dawson did not know the governor, nor were they the kind to care too much about "a seductive remark to an unnamed woman." Hickman attributed the assault to orders from Bob Golden, captain of the police, deputy sheriff, and constable of Salt Lake City. The seven accused claimed that Golden told them "to give the Governor a good beating."

According to Hickman, he posted bail for Jason Luce, who immediately left Salt Lake City. Both Jason and Hickman knew too much about the Dawson affair to appear in court, and together they headed for Montana. Somewhere along the way Jason found a stage-driving job with a company that linked Bannock City, Idaho, and Salt Lake City.

Others involved in the Dawson affair did not fair so well. Huntington vowed never to be taken alive and chose California as his destination. To insure a speedy departure he stole the fastest horse in the county, a thoroughbred named Brown Sal which belonged to John Bennion's son. He also stole three other horses. Huntington set out with Moroni Clawson and John P. Smith, all determined to avoid prosecution and possible incarceration. Huntington would have been wise to have stolen a less valuable horse than Brown Sal. A posse was organized in Taylorsville that included John Bennion, Samuel Bateman, John Irving, Orson Cutler, Porter Rockwell, and three others.

The posse followed the fugitives to the Rush Valley mail station, twenty-one miles west of Camp Floyd. At about 10 a.m., when Huntington stepped from the station, he was ordered to halt by Rockwell. Huntington hesitated only a moment, then tried to scale a nearby fence as he ran for a horse. Rockwell leveled his guns and shot him twice in the back. Huntington died hanging over the fence. Clawson and Smith escaped to Faust's Station, where they surrendered. They were placed in a wagon with

Huntington's body and brought into Salt Lake City to the police. But that night, while being escorted to jail by four guards, Clawson and Smith were shot to death, reportedly as "they tried to escape."

John Woodly, one of the four guards escorting Clawson and Smith to jail, and the only guard ever questioned about the shooting, asserted that the prisoners "made an attempt to escape, one running one way and the other the other and were shot." Hickman claimed he examined the two bodies and determined that Clawson and Smith had not been running away. "Both were powder-burnt, and one of them was shot in the face."

When the case of the beating of Governor Dawson came to court, only one defendant was found guilty. Wilford Luce was fined fifty dollars and sentenced to one year in the penitentiary. The full story of who ordered the beating of Dawson has not been determined.

– 13 –

The Morrisite Affair

During the summer of 1862, Bill Hickman traveled to Montana to look for gold and to pick up some horses he had purchased the year before from Bob Dempsey, a mountain man. Hickman was chosen leader of a group of forty-eight travelers from California, Colorado, and Utah, which included two of Hickman's "boys." On the return trip, Hickman writes, he persuaded "Irish Ned" to remain behind in Idaho to prospect a "worthless claim" he received from Hickman. Unexpectedly, Ned dug $42,000 worth of gold from the claim in one winter. No doubt Irish Ned's luck would haunt Hickman, who was watching his family edge further into poverty. "I went on home . . . found everything right, and was aiming to live at home and be quiet, attend to farm stock, and raise my family in peace," Hickman wrote of his return. He was determined "not ever . . . to again occupy any position in the church, or as an officer. I threshed my grain, and seldom went to town." He seemed to be reconciling himself to a more circumspect lifestyle and distancing himself from local church leaders.

Hickman reached Salt Lake City a few weeks before Colonel Patrick Edward Connor arrived from California at the head of his three to four hundred troops. With Camp Floyd destroyed, the feeling in the nation's capitol was that a U.S. Army presence of some kind was needed in Utah to insure that the Mormons did not try to secede from the Union. Connor's orders called for him to march the Third California Infantry and the Second California Cavalry to Utah in May 1862. He arrived in October. The people of Fairfield assumed the colonel would settle in their area as Johnston's Army had four years earlier, but Connor had other plans.

Hickman was still cocky enough to bet $500 that Connor would not be allowed to cross the Jordan River. On hearing of Hickman's bet, the colonel reportedly replied, "I will cross the River Jordan if hell yawns below me." He crossed on 18 October 1862 at 2:00 p.m. and headed straight for the East Bench overlooking Salt Lake City. A delegation was sent from church headquarters to assure Connor that they had not intended to impede his entry. Connor constructed a new fort on the bench and named it after former Illinois senator and defeated U.S. presidential candidate, Stephen A. Douglas. This choice must have annoyed Brigham Young, for Douglas had openly attacked the Saints in Illinois before his death.

Stephen S. Harding, President Abraham Lincoln's appointee for Utah territorial governor, arrived in the Salt Lake Valley two months before Connor. Both Harding and Connor were to become friends of Bill Hickman before the end of 1863, and these friendships would mark the beginning of Hickman's estrangement from Brigham Young.

Governor Harding arrived in the city in July 1862 and was surprised to find the Mormons unconcerned about the Civil War and the fate of the South. He felt this lack of concern masked a desire by Mormons to separate from the Union. Mormons were similarly unimpressed with Harding. On 4 March 1863, seven months after Harding's arrival, a notice ran in the *Deseret News* calling for a mass meeting to consider a petition asking for the new governor's removal. Before the summer was over Harding was on his way to Colorado as Chief Justice of the Colorado Supreme Court, where he would serve until 1868. His reception in Colorado would be equally cool, ending in the refusal of local lawyers to try their cases in his court.

What became known as the Morrisite Affair inflamed Mormon sentiment against Harding. Joseph Morris, a British convert to Mormonism, declared that God had called him to be a new prophet in place of Brigham Young. He backed up his claim by telling of angelic visitations. Morris believed in the communal ownership of property. All of his converts were required to relinquish their properties to his "United Order." After several months, followers William Jones, John Jensen, and Lewis C. Gurson decided they wanted to leave Morris and reclaim their property. Because Morris, like Young, believed in blood atonement, the three men were captured, brought back, and threatened. By this time Morris had a following of more than five hundred.

Armed with writs of arrest and with guns, Salt Lake City sheriff Robert T. Burton, a Mormon and close confidant of Brigham Young, headed with a posse of more than five hundred men toward the Weber River on the morning of 13 June 1862. Mormon settlers lined the road north, cheering the posse on its way. Morris had gathered his impoverished group together near the river, promising them "in the name of God, that bullets and cannon would not harm them, as they were under God's hand." Burton demanded that Morris and the others surrender. He then reportedly fired at Morris, exclaiming, "I will try your God." Within thirty minutes, seventeen Morrisites, including Morris and Joseph Banks, his assistant, were dead. Two from Burton's posse were also dead, for which seven Morrisite men would be convicted of second-degree murder on 7 March 1863.

Colonel Connor offered to escort between sixty and eighty Morrisite families to Soda Springs, Idaho, where they could safely pursue their religious beliefs. They left Utah on 5 May 1863 with Company H, the Third California Infantry. Hickman acted as guide. Other Morrisites relocated in Nevada, California, and Montana. Those remaining in Utah agreed to abandon their religion.

Many Mormons may have privately felt the Morrisites should have been left alone to follow their beliefs, but few expressed public support for the sect. Bill Hickman was an exception. He reportedly rode thirty miles to sign a petition to Harding, asking him to pardon the seven Morrisites in prison, and also called Sherrif Burton "a dog."

Burton was not arrested for the Morrisite murders until August 1876. Finally, Burton gave himself up. He was tried and acquitted by a jury of Mormons and non-Mormons on 20 February 1879, seventeen years after the event. According to Orson F. Whitney, Burton's acquittal marked "the cessation of the vexatious proceedings . . . robbing the graves of the past in order to harass and annoy reputable citizens against whom no crime could be proved." Less than two weeks after the Morrisite massacre, Hickman wrote a letter to Brigham Young:

> I expect to leave in a few days and may not have a chance to leave you a line. My confidence in you is unshaken, your council to me [has] always been good, and I delight in it. When I think I have your confidence it wipes away all troubles and sorrow, and I do hope that I may so live that I may enjoy your society in time and all eternity. O! how I wish that I could be thrown in some position where I could see you every day.

Pleasantries aside, Hickman proceeded to fill his letter with complaints against Archibald Gardner, Hickman's bishop, who had set out to find evidence that Hickman was still stealing cattle and horses:

> He [Gardner] raked the river in a most exulting manner. Bringing 26 men, and tried to get more, reproving men who said, they would find [their] Bros. cattle and hides.
>
> One man bet a cow they will find, even shakes hands on it. I have not been mobbed in a long time. Before the spirit of it was down rite mobacracy as was ever thrown around me. Sparing, running, jumping, wrestling, pitching horse shoes, drinking whiskey etc. With every damnable look at me that was ever cast by a mob. Has sought every occasion to bring destruction upon me—I know not why unless to aggrandize himself.
>
> It does not seem to be his aim to be down on thieves—for I have pointed out thieves and told him how he could get hold of them, but he has not made a move against one of them. They seem to be his intimate friends.
>
> I wish to be released from his jurisdiction. Your word is law to me. May the Lord bless forever.

Although Gardner used force to search Hickman's property, he found nothing. This incident, along with the Morrisite Affair, seems to have convinced Hickman that isolation would not guarantee safety, and he again began to spend less time at home working the farm.

On 10 December 1862, Hickman wrote another letter to Young:

> I have sought an opportunity to see you several times recently. I now have to go home and thought it wou[ld] be well to leave a line for you—I am solicited to visit Judges, the Gov. and the offices at Camp, and confer with them on what

course was best to pursue in this Territory etc. I have been assured that there was bound to be trouble here. I have kept myself aloff from all of them up to a few days since. I would like to know what you would like me to [do]. To continue my interview or to let them pass and keep away from them. Your will shall be my pleasure. I am not the Jud[g]e of this or even myself—

In early December 1863 Jason Luce, Hickman's brother-in-law returned to Salt Lake City. Luce had been working on a stage line during the past two years. He was immediately charged with "knifing to death one Samuel Bunton of Oregon, newly arrived in the city of Salt Lake." The police investigation revealed that Luce had known Bunton in Bannock City, Idaho, and Bunton "had attacked him, mal-treated, kicked and trampled him, and threatened him with a knife." Bunton, it was reported, had owed money to the express company for which Jason was a driver.

On 15 December, eight days after Bunton's death, the grand jury of the probate court returned an indictment for murder against Luce. The trial began on 16 December, with "W. A. Hickman Esq." identified as "counsel for the prisoner." Thirteen days later, the court sentenced Luce to be "shot till dead, within the courthouse yard," on 12 January. Hickman did everything he could to procure a commutation of sentence but was unsuccessful and Luce was executed. Within days of the execution a letter arrived at the *Deseret News* signed by a group of Bannock County citizens, proclaiming, "Samuel Bunton is a murderer, and a desperado. If he had not been killed in Salt Lake City by Jason Luce, Bannock citizens would have done him in."

Two months later, the *Deseret News* carried an account of Luce's final hours: "On the appointed day and for some days preceeding, Jason showed much contrition of heart for the latter years of his life—he warned young men against bad associates and attested he had been 'betrayed unto death' by one of his counsel." The article concluded didactically, "The end of Jason might have been vastly different had he only 'avoided evil associates,' for he was a fine hard working man."

Apparently, Luce had turned against Hickman in the end. According to Wilford Woodruff, who had been a Luce family friend for years, Luce "said he was innocent of many things that the people thought him guilty of Said he had never killed any person or had any part in the death of any person, except Rhodes and Bunton—he was not guilty, had killed in self-defense. He said Wm. Hickman aroused him to do many things that made his flesh creep but he had not followed Hickman's advice in these things."

Woodruff asked Luce to relate the details of Drown's and Arnold's deaths. According to Woodruff, Luce claimed that "Hickman was responsible for their deaths. He killed them with the help of 1 or 2 others." Luce continued, saying that

> Hickman murdered [blank] for no other purpose than to obtain his gold watch and money and thinks he has the watch yet. Hickman was at the head of a band of thieves that had stolen as high as 100 head of cattle from Camp Floyd and gone out on the praire and divided them. He has many men around him that need to be fed, these men steal cattle which they kill and eat, and make lariats. Hickman has been my ruin and the ruin of others.

According to Luce, Hickman had told him that "Brigham Young had given him counsel to do all these things."

The day of the execution Brigham Young wrote the following in his journal:

> Jason Luce executed at noon. His mother, brother [John Martin Luce], wife and five children visited him last night and this morning. He requested his brother to take care of a woman he had impregnated. He confessed all his sins and asked God for forgiveness. He addressed the people from his chair—feet manacled—pronounced Wm. Hickman his betrayer, he bid the people goodby. His face was covered, 5 balls shot into his heart—no groan.

Luce's execution marked the end of an era. Four from Hickman's "gang" were dead, and two—Wilford Luce and Samuel Butcher—were in prison. Based on Luce's death-bed confession, city lawmen decided to watch Hickman's house. They also put men on the road out of Salt Lake City to monitor his movements when he left town. Four years later they would trail him to Wyoming while he mined gold. Increasingly paranoid, Hickman was convinced their objective was to kill him.

– 14 –

Government Guide

The Gentiles may have welcomed Bill Hickman into their camp, but Hickman was hoping to straddle the fence—to make a living where he could without breaking with church leaders. Such an approach would prove impossible in 1863.

His friendship with Patrick Connor brought him badly needed employment. Connor was made a brigadier general in 1863 and hired Hickman as a guide and "Indian spy" between May 1863 and December 1865. Hickman's pay was usually $150 per month. His last government pay voucher was issued on 6 December 1865 for $30.

His friendship with Connor also led to his involvement in Utah mining. Connor reportedly asked Hickman whether he had "any scruples about prospecting because of Brigham Young's advice against it." Assuring him he did not, Hickman reported, "I brought him a good piece of Galena ore from Bingham Canyon, which was the start of mining in Utah." Connor saw mining as the key to money and power in the Utah territory. "Give us the gold and silver," he reportedly said, "and before long all the Mormons will be working for us." Connor also regarded himself as a savior of sorts of the local people. His newspaper, The Union Vedette, the first daily in the territory, barely concealed his mistaken belief that the Mormons were anxiously awaiting deliverance from their powerful church leaders.

After examining the rich ore Hickman brought from Bingham Canyon, Connor met with Bishop Archibald Gardner about forming a mining district in the West Jordan area. The meeting was held at Gardner's Grist Mill. Twenty-five men were invited to attend and become the first shareholders. Each shareholder held 200 feet in the canyon and was required one day per month to work or the share could be "jumped." The West Jordan Mining District was formally organized on 17 September, as was a company called the Jordan Silver Mining Company. Eight of those in attendance were officers from Fort Douglas, friends of General Connor.

Bill Hickman did not get rich on mining. He helped organize a number of other small, private mining districts and mines for property owners in the west valley. No doubt he charged for his legal services, but this was probably the extent of his wealth as the "mining bubble" soon burst for him. As he wrote in 1871, "I have located and helped others who have made nice sums of money, but many instances have been neglected."

Brigham Young distrusted men who accepted government employment and advised Hickman twice during the summer of 1863 to leave Connor's employ and, as Hickman puts it, to "kidnap Connor, the Irish Ditcher, and send him over into California." Young, according to Hickman, offered $1,000, plus all expenses. "I stood up to Brigham for the first time ever, and said I would not do it," Hickman wrote, "for General Connor was a good man, and the best officer ever in Utah." As Hickman saw it, "I was in the Government employ, and all hands had set to break me up, stigmatize, even kill me for taking the course I did in rendering Government official help." But Hickman wanted to remain a Mormon. He continued to cultivate communication with Young, hoping to retain his favor.

During July 1863 Hickman participated in one of the final Indian skirmishes in the mountains east of Provo. The event was chronicled in the *Deseret News*, one headline reading "Sinister Hickman." The superintendent of Indian affairs, a federal appointee, had given more land to Chief Little Soldier than Mormon settlers in Utah County believed he was entitled to, especially where the grant encroached on Mormon land near Point of the Mountain. Conflict between the settlers and the Indians developed, and Connor ordered twenty-five of his troops from Fort Douglas to the area to protect the overland mail and telegraph routes. The officer in charge challenged Little Soldier to battle. After a brief encounter, many of the Indians escaped to the mountains east of the lake, and additional troops were sent for.

The increased regiment could not locate Little Soldier and instead attacked a docile band of Utah Indians near Spanish Fork.

Among the dead were Indians and soldiers both. The Indians then attacked the mail coach, killing the driver and one other individual. Hickman and Connor, recently returned from Soda Springs, immediately took charge. Connor recalled:

> Mr. Hickman, who had, as stated, been in the employ of the Government for some time previous, in various capacities, as an ambassador or minister plenipotentiary and extraordinary to effect a cessation of hostilities with the bands reported to be marshalling for war in the mountains surrounding Utah Valley. Mr. Hickman . . . turned his attention to Little Soldier, who was in the Battle Creek hills . . . with meat and about 25 or so bucks. Mr. Hickman reported, 'the Indians want assurance of peace not extermination.' Mr. Hickman returned to the city for some blankets for presents to the Indians, in order to convince them he was not talking 'forked,' and trying to entrap them. It is hoped that the peace policy which has of late been adopted will be followed out . . . and not many weeks will pass . . . that a treaty of peace and amnity have been made with all the bands which have of late been stirred to war.

A letter to the *Deseret News* in July 1863 by second lieutenant Anthony Ethier of the Second Cavalry Volunteers, underscored Hickman's failure to negotiate peace: "I was shot on first by 100 Indians led by the late 'Little Soldier.'" Ethier reported that Chief Little Soldier was killed, and believed that the constant misrepresentations of the whites should be stopped. "[It is] understood by people everywhere," he continued, "that it is not the policy of the *leaders* in this community to have peace made with the Indians."

Hickman's involvement with General Connor continued through the winter of 1864, when Connor asked Hickman to help in the location of twelve mules that had disappeared from Rush Valley. The mules were discovered, along with the men who had stolen them, and an additional "several thousand dollars worth of stolen goods." Hickman reported this to Sheriff Burton, who allowed Hickman to lead a small posse out to arrest the men. Reward money of $500 had been posted for the return of the stolen goods, and Hickman tried to collect the $500 several days later. Instead he was arrested for complicity in the theft. Bail was set at $130,000. Hickman managed through friends to raise the bail. He was furious with the sheriff and his men—"a blacker set of scamps I never knew"—and claimed Burton was "Brigham's dirty-jobber, and has been for eight or ten years."

According to the same indictments, George Heath, James Rhodes, and Louis Dauganser had stolen coats, hats, boots, and blankets from N. S. Ransohff's store and Hickman had given "counsel, advice, and assistance in said crime." Heath, Rhodes, and Dauganser pleaded guilty. A grand jury found that "after the stolen items were carried away, on October 25, 1864 in Little Cottonwood Canyon, one William A. Hickman, did unlawfully buy and receive from John Nelson and others a large quantity of the stolen goods, knowing said goods were stolen . . . and a great quantity of other items."

Hickman claimed he was in military service at the time and "therefore was subject to the rules and regulations and articles of war, and could not be tried by civil authority." The judge was not persuaded and proceeded with the trial. But the case was dismissed several days later.

Hickman wrote to Brigham Young on 7 January 1865 complaining of his arrest, calling it a raid on his integrity:

> I will not lay down and be still against those who unjustly try to injure. I will not die as a skunk . . . My God, I know my innocense and I believe you know it. Such hellish treatment to me by spies and dogs hounding me is more than I can or will stand any longer. If I have done anything unpleasant to you or contrary to your wishes I am sorry from the bottom of my heart and am ready to make any restitution.

Young was not pleased with Hickman's letter but replied, "I do have objections to your making capitol out of the interviews which I grant you; but call and see me when you are here." Then: "I have said, publicly and privately, that I had no sympathy with men who meddle with things which are not their own and take that which belongs to others. So far as I can learn, however, there is no evidence against you for wrong-doing in this case, except the testimony of those criminals whose statements cannot be heard as evidence."

After the meeting with Young, Hickman would write to him again on 25 April 1865:

> It has been some time since I have seen you or wrote to you. I saw you, you convinced me to raise corn and wheat. I went to work, have worked very hard ever since. I find that

my labors will not support my family without doing some other business and let every bodies else alone, but I find the town officials are in a rage again, determined to bring some trouble and destruction on me. They say that just as soon as they can find something to put me under arrest that they will use me up and put an end to me—I know of no crime or offence that I have committed. I have done the best I knew.

I have violated no covenants nor betrayed a single confidence so far as these things are concerned. I have been light as a drum [i.e., sober]—anything that is said to the reverse is false as hell. I am tired of having to always be on the look out, being annoyed, and in danger of my life. I wish I could have peace. I wish we had good honest and truthful men in office. If you want me to do anything, just let me know it.

If you want me to go aways I will go. If you want this or that, or whatever you may think, I will try. Or if you want my life you can have it without a murmur or a groan, just let me know late or early. I will be there, and there will be no tale left behind. What more can I say. What more can I do. I am on hand. Now, when I say this to you, I do not mean any of those who have for the last four or five years sought my destruction. I will never yield a hair if I can help it to them. I remember my covenants, but they do not. I seek not their destruction, but they do mine. If it were not for those obligations I am under, things would be different.

P. S. I would like you to keep this and not let any know of it. Use your own council and I am satisfied.

Hickman was poor, and his son-in-law Samuel Monroe Butcher was in worse condition. Butcher, a rough, uneducated man, also had difficulty finding a legitimate means of support for his large family. His wife, Sarah Katharine Hickman, bore him eleven children before she was thirty years old. On 4 January, the case, "The People vs. Samuel M. Butcher," came to court. Butcher was found guilty and sentenced to "three years hard labor at the Utah Penitentiary, and fined $300.00." Butcher served only fourteen months, when he was pardoned, though in the interim Bill accepted the additional burden of feeding and caring for his daughter and grandchildren.

Hickman had appeared on the ward tithing records from 1851 through November 1864, when all payments to the church ceased. He asserted that Bishop Gardner and others had begun encouraging his wives to leave him. The Horr sisters were the first to go. Because Hickman cherished his children and wives, he considered Gardner's advice an assault on him and his family.

It is not surprising that Hickman considered moving back to Missouri. Minerva Lerona recalled that her "Pa wanted to take his family and go, the first family all wanted to go." The other wives and children convinced him to discard this notion. Such a move would have probably aggravated his mounting debts and family troubles.

From 19 July to 6 December 1865, Hickman worked full time for Connor as a guide in "the west subdivision of the Plains." From the description on his pay vouchers, he was employed as a "guide for troops and a spy and detective" on the Indians. On 7 December 1865 a message arrived from Washington: "The General Commanding directs that W. A. Hickman, guide, be discharged from the Service of the United States."

Playing one leader against the other and hoping for forgiveness for past disloyalties could not have lasted forever. Now Hickman had lost the confidence of both government and church. He would either have to regain the trust of the one or the other, or consider moving out of the territory once and for all.

– 15 –

The RLDS in Utah

Joseph Smith's sons Joseph III, Alexander, and David, separately or together, visited Utah at least five times between 1866 and 1876, hoping to convince Brigham Young that their father had never sanctioned polygamy. Their aim was to bring Utah Mormons back to "the true church," the Reorganized Church of Jesus Christ of Latter Day Saints. During their 1869 visit, David and Alexander asked Young to let them preach in the Tabernacle. He refused. Hickman wrote that he went to visit the Smiths during their stay "out of respect to their father."

The RLDS mission to Salt Lake City won approximately 3,000 converts; most left Utah for Missouri. Minerva Lerona remembered that her father "wanted to go. The Josephites was so strong it seemed like one-third of the people went back east with General Connor's offer to take them."

Hickman was accused by both Brigham Young and his daughter Kitten of joining the "Josephites," but there is no proof he was ever baptized. The charge later brought against him by Brigham Young in 1868 was that of "Being intimate with the Smith boys, Joseph's sons, when they were in town." Apparently "Uncle" John Smith, a cousin of Alexander Smith, accompanied Hickman to see the Smiths in 1866, because during Hickman's 1868 interview with Young, John Smith was called to testify on Hickman's behalf. Hickman says that Young "was disposed not to believe him." Much later, another son, Joseph Smith III, wrote about Hickman after his own visit to Utah:

> I believed that while bearing the awful reputation which developed as a result of his deeds, the man did really grow tired of the criminal life he was leading, and that, repenting of his wickedness, he would have sought refuge in the true Church had he had the courage to take the step. That he did not unite with us was due, I was told to the fact that in conversation with some of our elders . . . he got the idea that according to the legendary teaching of the authorities of the church, such repentance was entirely futile and that it would be useless for him, a murderer, to be baptized.

Hickman's last child had been born in 1865 to his third wife, Minerva, while Hickman was on guide duty for Connor's troops at the time. A son had been born seven months before to Mary Jane, his tenth wife. There were now nineteen children under ten years of age tended by seven wives.

During the winter of 1866-67 word came that Tom Ryan had discovered gold on the Sweetwater River in Wyoming territory. Hickman applied to Brigham Young for a pass out of the Utah territory, which was granted on 4 June 1867:

> To Whom It May Concern: I understand that Brother William Hickman is intending to leave this Territory, and in view of his doing so he should be at liberty to go on to the Range and gather up his stock and do other legitimate business that may be necessary to his departure. He informs me that some persons have been threatening him. This should not be. I know of no reason why he should not be permitted to attend to his business and leave, when he gets ready, in peace and quietness.

Hickman left Utah along with Captain J. W. Lawrence, Porter Rockwell and others heading towards South Pass and the gold fields. Hickman and others found the Carissa Lode and filed a claim in Laramie. The large mining tipple they built still stands, abandoned and useless, at the top of Mormon Gulch in South Pass City, Wyoming.

According to Hickman, a ten-mile trip into the mountains around South Pass City convinced him Indian troubles were brewing—a fear he reported back to the camp of some 150 miners. The miners had little enthusiasm for preparing themselves against an uncertain threat. Hickman and ten others decided to leave the camp for Salt Lake City, fearing a hostile attack. The day after Hickman left, a party of Sioux Indians attacked the newly constructed mine, killing three men and scattering the others. Captain Lawrence was one of the three killed. According to Hickman, some of the fleeing men overtook his party before they reached the Green River sixty-nine miles away.

Back home, Hickman had no job, and he had sold his Taylorsville property to finance his mining venture. He now bought a small ranch at the mouth of Bingham Canyon and, as he wrote, moved "my family and stock there, built a good corral, and commenced to improve . . . but to my sorrow, I soon saw that I was again watched; men were prowling around day and night." Hickman felt the necessity once again to leave the territory. He left in October, telling his pursuers that he was searching for lost animals. He rode west across the mountains, avoiding roads or trails, finally stopping to rest at Deep Creek, Nevada, two hundred miles to the west. His destination was Austin, Nevada, where several old acquaintances resided.

In August Hickman received letters from his family advising him not to return home. Two weeks later, a man came into Austin and reported that three policemen had followed him as far as Deep Creek, claiming they were searching for Hickman for the unsolved 1866 murder of J. King Robinson.

During the fall, five of Hickman's remaining eight wives would leave him. Some eventually married other men; others moved in with relatives or became self-supporting. Minerva later wrote about the decision to break up the family:

> In 1867 we all agreed to break-up the marriage relationship, that is the polygamous ties joining us together. Each one going for ourselves and doing the best we could for our children. Hickman was as generous as he could afford to be with each wife. He gave me a yoke of oxen and a wagon, 2 cows worth $150.00, a span of mules, two colts, and 100 pounds of flour.

Minerva moved to North Ogden to live with her brother, Edward Wade. Her oldest child, Bill Hickman, Jr., was seventeen years old; her youngest, Mary Ella, only two. Her brother eventually built Minerva a house across the road from his home. She took her loom with her to North Ogden but "quit weaving, too hard, and went to midwifery." She eventually delivered 352 babies from North Ogden to Pocatello, Idaho, before she retired in 1902. Minerva was thirty-nine years old when she left in 1867. To her death she insisted, "He was the only man I ever loved."

Hickman decided to go on to San Francisco, where he found his "old and true friend, General Connor." Connor had left his Fort Douglas post and gone back to California in March 1866 without an official release or explanation. Hickman found that Connor had become successful in business and asked Connor to send a letter to Brigham Young stating that Hickman had never disclosed Mormon secrets to Connor. If the letter was written and mailed, it has since been lost.

Hickman was undecided about what he should do. With Connor in San Francisco and Young still smarting over Hickman's overtures to the Smith brothers, he was as yet unreconciled to either government or church—his former sources of income. He considered sailing from San Francisco to New York and taking the railroad from there to western Missouri, where he might send for his remaining family. But in the end he decided to return to Nevada. Letters from home were waiting for Hickman when he reached Carson City advising him to come back, that things had quieted down and that it would be safe. Brigham Young counseled his son to write to him and say, "Come home."

Hickman answered at least one of Minerva's letters from Carson City. He was still thinking about taking his family with him and was blaming others for his troubles. Whether or not he was able yet to grasp the reality of his relationship to his alienated wives, his unwavering love for his children and wives was touching:

> Dear Minerva,
>
> I have often thought of you and the little fellows. O! how I want to see them. I wish you all the good I can, and hope you are well and doing well—I saw Sarah's man, and that is Wm. Frances accidentally. They were just going to start over the mountains but on meeting me they stayed a day longer. It was very surprising to me to meet them as I had not heard of their being married neither had I any idea of it. . . . Now, Minerva it depends on you to do right, and we will loose none of our children but will have them and enjoy their society, but you do talk so strange and so bad in your letters—about that reckless old father to your child—I don't know what to think. I have not talked about you, nor felt bad towards you, and hoped you would hold on and we would soon be together in peace—that reckless father, Minerva. What am I reckless

in? I know nothing but getting out of the clutches of those who have robbed me of pretty near our all, as you very well know, what went with our cattle killed and eat money unjustly taken, hundred of dollars, and then my life sought, and I was reckless for not suffering them to kill me. O! foolish woman you surely don't think—but I forgive you and hope you will rightly consider things hereafter. Minerva do right and don't be wrongly persuaded by any person, live humble and prayerful and the Lord will bless you—kiss all the children for me and tell them Pa loves them and wants to see them and you tell them you will take them where Pa and Sarah's man is after a while not here but East—Minerva do right.

Minerva decided not to "do right" and left the Salt Lake Valley for north Ogden.

That winter Hickman also wrote to Brigham Young. This letter, like Connor's letter to Young, cannot be found, but its contents can be surmised from the angry reply Young sent to Hickman in Carson City on 22 January 1868. Whatever else Hickman wrote, he must have threatened to "disclose all." Young's answer invited him to say anything he wished. The letter ends with Young quoting, "The wicked fleeth when no man pursueth," and advised Hickman to return to Utah and his family, the "best place for your temporal and spiritual salvation."

Hickman disregarded Young's invitation to return to Utah and attempted instead to do freighting work between Carson City and Placerville, California. He found the work too much of a strain on his bad leg and had to quit. Hickman called the unresponsive muscles and recurring inflammation in his thigh "typhoid sickness." His leg "swelled to the size of a common flour sack," and his friends who saw it were sure he was going to die. He lay in the cabins of friends and strangers throughout western Nevada. After four months of extreme suffering, he was finally able to catch the stage from Virginia City, Nevada, for Salt Lake City.

Hickman returned to Utah in July or August 1868, one or two months after his excommunication. Without a bishop's court, trial, or stated complaint, he was denied his church membership on 12 June 1868. He found only three wives waiting for him in Fairfield: his first wife, Bernetta, with no children at home; Sarah Basford, his fourth, with four under the age of twelve; and his tenth, Mary Jane Hetherington, with two young boys three and seven years old. The others had left. And Sarah Basford would marry John Franks within days of Hickman's return.

Mary Jane posed a larger problem. She had no family or relatives to take her in and Hickman was unable and unwilling to support her. An orphan when she married Hickman, she now had to find a means of support again for herself and her two young sons. At twenty-eight, she had few options. She finally became a laundress for the miners in Stockton, Utah, at General Connor's new mining community. Later she opened a boarding house for miners and supported herself and her boys by washing and cooking. To her granddaughter years later she commented, "It was backbreaking work," as she complained of hand-washing the excessively dirty clothes of the miners.

Hickman had at least four interviews with Brigham Young after his return to Salt Lake City. The first two concerned his excommunication. Hickman wanted to find the reason for the action; Young offered to send a letter of recommendation to Bishop Gardner that Hickman be rebaptized. The last two interviews concerned business. No doubt Hickman was trying to get work with Young's railroad contract. But both men were irreconcilably hardened towards each other. Hickman needed money and work. Young wanted confession and contrition. Neither man would take an openly hostile stance toward the other, nor would either capitulate.

On 15 August 1868, Hickman wrote for the last time to Young. Hickman's entire letter read:

> Dear Brigham, I feel bad to have so many false charges brought against me, I feel bad when I think you do not feel well towards me. What am I to do when I do not know of wrong I have done, how or of what can I repent I wish you would point out a coarse [sic] and have it under your immediate notice for me to take, not under Gardner I asked you once to release me from his jurisdiction and understood you had. I hope you will remember me and do me justice. I ask nothing more.
>
> Wm. A. Hickman
>
> I know I was always your friend at home or aboard and true in every sense of the word. I do hope you'll be kind to me—how bad I feel you do not know.

No answer was received. Hickman claimed that he saw Young several times thereafter and that Young would always ask, "When are you going to be baptized again and join the church?" Hickman wanted an apology and reinstatement without rebaptism.

Hickman went to Tooele to again work church stock in Rush Valley. He was hired by Bryant Stringham, but when Young heard about this, Stringham was "dressed down" for hiring a "gentile," and Hickman was fired.

The only work he could find was drawing up mining claims for Fairfield and Tooele county residents. He also acted as counsel for the defense in several legal cases in Tooele County between 1868 and 1870. He organized the Camp Floyd Mining District, called a meeting, and introduced residents to the intricacies of mining laws and district constitutions. However, the mining work was shortlived, and Hickman, unemployed, was left with only his small house and piece of land in Fairfield.

– 16 –

The Murder of "Spanish Frank"

A family crisis faced Hickman following his return home in mid-1868. Sarah Elizabeth Virginia Johnson, the daughter of former Mormon apostle Luke Johnson and Hickman's former wife, had married a "black Spaniard" and taken Hickman's four children with her into the new marriage.

Hickman was upset by the gossip about Frank Moreno, "Spanish Frank," and his former wife and family. They were living in an isolated cabin in the Oquirrh Mountains, away from church, schools, and town. Reports were filtering into Tooele and Fairfield that Moreno had eyes for his step-daughter, Laura Isbella, only eleven years old. Hickman decided to take Moreno and Sarah Virginia to court and demand custody of his four children. On 27 September 1870, he filed a legal complaint in the Tooele Probate Court. The judge, not a friend of Hickman, nevertheless awarded custody of the children to him. The judge gave Moreno and Sarah ten days to deliver the children to Hickman and required a $500 compliance bond to be left with the court. The couple pleaded poverty, and Hickman paid the bond for them.

At the end of the ten days, Hickman sent a friend in a wagon to pick up the children. After Hickman's friend had signed the receipt of delivery, Sarah, in league with Moreno, called to the children to jump from the wagon and run back to the house.

Four or five days later someone knocked on the door of the cabin late at night. Moreno opened the door, was felled by "a dozen buckshot," and dropped dead. Hickman never admitted to firing the gun, but family stories attributed the shooting to Hickman. According to some descendants, Sarah left Utah and married Edwin Sherman, a non-Mormon who owned a funeral parlor in Butte, Montana.

On 12 October 1870, Hickman was indicted for Moreno's murder in Salt Lake City's third district court. Hickman had disappeared into the Oquirrh Mountains after learning of the indictment. Crippled and old, he was becoming less able to survive in the mountains. The infection in his hip wound returned: "I was taken with the typhoid fever, and, as it served me three years before, it fell into my lame thigh, and in twenty hours it was so swollen that I could not walk. In this situation I remained until I had it lanced, but was not able to walk for two months. I was hauled home, and then to other places until I got well enough to ride around."

During this 1870-71 winter of sickness, Hickman heard that Deputy Marshall H. Gilson was searching for him in earnest. Hickman's son George arranged a meeting between the two on 15 April 1871, sixteen miles west of Nephi. Gilson came with a deal: Hickman's life in exchange for his testimony against Brigham Young. It was an offer Hickman felt he could not refuse.

In August 1870 James McKean arrived in Utah to become chief justice of the territorial supreme court and judge of the third judicial district. McKean felt "called" to his appointment and arrived in the territory anxious to take on Brigham Young. On one occasion, the judge stated: "The mission which God has called upon me to perform in Utah, is as much above the duties of other courts and judges as the heavens are above the earth, and whenever or wherever I may find the Local or Federal laws obstructing or interfering therewith, by God's blessing I shall trample them under my feet."

McKean had barely donned his judicial robes in Utah when he read about the murder of "Spanish Frank." The report of Frank Moreno's death appeared on the front page of the *Deseret News* on 12 October 1870 under the headline, "Murder in Rush Valley." Bill Hickman's reputation was so widely known that no newspaper reader needed further identification beyond "The Notorious" to identify Hickman as the culprit. An indictment for Hickman's arrest was issued by McKean's third district court the same day.

Learning more of Hickman's background, McKean became convinced that this man, who had once been a close friend of Brigham Young, could be of use.

Hickman was exonerated of murder charges in March 1871, and in September a grand jury was convened to hear the testimony of Bill Hickman and John Flack, a former member of Bill's gang, regarding Brigham Young's involvement in the murder of the arms dealer, Yates.

On 19 September, Albert Carrington, who would later become a Mormon apostle but was then editor of the *Deseret News*, wrote of his experience on being called to serve on the grand jury and being questioned by prosecuting attorney R. N. Baskin.

Baskin: "Are you a member of the Church of Jesus Christ of Latter-day Saints?"

Carrington: "I am."

Baskin: "Is not polygamy one of the fundamental doctrines of that church?"

Carrington: "Plurality of wives is a doctrine of the Church."

Baskin: "Do you believe the revelation which teaches this doctrine to the church to be from God and binding upon his people?"

Carrington: "I do."

Baskin: "Which do you believe ought to be obeyed, the revelation or the law?"

Carrington: "I do not think the question a proper one."

Baskin: "Do you not think the revelation superior to law?"

Carrington: "My views on this are known through my public utterances."

Baskin: "Do you believe that a man in marrying more than one wife commits adultery?"

Carrington: "I do not, if he marries them according to the revelation."

Baskin: "You do not believe this to be adultery?"

Carrington: "I do not."

At this point, Carrington was dismissed as a prospective juror. Others with similar views were also dismissed. To those remaining Baskin announced: "If there are any of you who believe that a man who has more than one wife does not commit adultery stand up." All remained seated. None were Mormon.

Unfortunately, the court record for 18 September 1871 is not available. Only newspaper accounts exist, including the following:

> *Daily Gate City [Keokuk, Iowa],* 24 September 1871: Excitement in Utah—The Mormons are said to be preparing to resist the U.S. officers. The grand Jury has adjourned until Tuesday. There are exciting rumors that high dignitaries of the Mormon Church are to be indicted . . . the Mormon Militia said to be drilling at night.

> *Daily Gate City,* 26 September 1871: Before going to Tooele the First Presidency learned that an alliance had been formed between the U.S. Ring here and Wm. A. Hickman and his band of thieves. Hickman was arrested sometime since on a charge of murder in the first degree. He has been told that if he would criminate the leading authorities of the Church on some capitol crime, he would be exonerated from guilt and probably receive some consideration; although charged with murder committed about a year ago with contestable evidence, he has been at large on parole on his own verbal recognizance.

The *Deseret News* of 11 October 1871 reported angrily:

> McKean is a New York export of a broken down and disappointed man. His appointment as Chief Justice of Utah was in the nature of a miraculous resurrection from the dead . . . He was scarcely warm in his seat before he was recognized as head of a conspiracy to destroy the peace, raze the institutions, and if possible take the lives of selected victims in the Mormon leadership . . . The drag-net of religious hate and political ambition was spread out for those, who, parties to former schisms and conflicts in the Mormon Church, confessed murderers and desperadoes, whose homes and prey were in the mountains, and similar wretches, *who to save their own lives*, or to wreck long cherished revenges, could be induced to swear away the lives of the best men whom we have ever known.
> The Notorious Bill Hickman, a self-confessed murderer, whose hands are said to be red with the blood of many innocent victims, is the boon companion, as well as the tool of these Utah conspirators.
> It is presumed to be on his and kindred testimony that Brigham Young, and other leading Mormons have been

indicted for murder. But all the Hickman hell-hounds and Morrisite outlaws which McKean, and Baskin, his attorney, can fish up from the lower depths of infamy cannot convince tens of thousands who know those men . . .

Three indictments were recorded on the criminal docket on 18 November 1871: "1. The People vs. Wm. Adams Hickman; indictment for murder; 2. The People vs. Brigham Young, Daniel H. Wells, Hosea Stout, William Adams Hickman, and Joseph A. Young; for murder; and 3. The People vs. Brigham Young, Wm. A. Hickman, Morris Meacham, Simon Dalton, George D. Grant, O. Porter Rockwell, and William Kimball, for murder." Young and Wells pleaded not guilty, and their cases were ordered continued until March 1872.

To his daughter, Katharine Hickman Butcher, Hickman told the truth when he wrote on 7 January 1872 from the Fort Douglas prison: "I have written a rough book, but no more rough than true." All of the indicted men except Young and Wells were incarcerated at the prison. Hickman, under protective custody, had been approached by James H. Beadle, western correspondent for the *Cincinnati Commercial*, about detailing his experiences with Young in a book, which he finished in prison. The majority of the manuscript had already been dictated secretly to Beadle and Alvira Barney, a local school teacher, before the indictment was served. Hickman would soon say that Beadle, not Hickman, was author of the book. But Hickman's letter from prison reflected the sentiment of the manuscript: "They say I am a traitor. Who is the traitor—when last fall I was accused of killing a desperado Spaniard who had taken my wife while I was run off [to California] by those murderers four years ago [1867], and he the villain making his brags how he intended to seduce my daughter."

According to William Kimball, Hickman began to deny authorship of his book while still in prison. After several unsuccessful attempts, he managed to speak to Kimball and said, "My book is a lie from the wild boar story onward." The wild boar story was on page 29—near the front.

After pleading not guilty, Young had gone to St. George in southern Utah for his annual winter vacation. While he was gone, the prosecuting attorney Baskin declared before the court that "Brigham Young is a fugitive from justice and will never again be seen in Salt Lake City, unless brought to the city by officers of the law." When this report reached Young, he made the long, cold trip from St. George to Salt Lake. He was past seventy-one years of age and feeble. When he arrived, he was placed under house arrest from 2 January 1872 to 29 April 1872.

Church lawyers challenged the legality of the court proceedings to the U.S. Supreme Court, which ruled in early 1872 that attempts by Gentile lawyers and judges in the territory to limit juries exclusively to the Gentiles—who constituted only 3 percent of Utah's population—infringed Mormon constitutional rights. All of the imprisoned Mormon men were freed, after six months of incarceration. On 29 April the *Tribune* reported "Brigham's Confession" to the government and the community. In a spirit of peace and reconciliation, Young had said, "Let us have peace for we have both been in the wrong and have run the great risk of destroying each other." Young was able to deliver the closing sermon at April's semi-annual General Conference, appearing in the tabernacle as a free man.

In 1875, after numerous complaints, Judge McKean was finally removed from office and from the territory. The Mormons appeared to have weathered another storm. However, polygamy and other issues would resurface periodically to plague the Saints until they finally conformed to federal law.

Hickman appears to have faded from sight after his prison release. In the summer of 1875, he was briefly in the limelight when he was asked by Governor George B. Emery to be one of the guards to escort John D. Lee of Mountain Meadows massacre fame from Beaver City to Salt Lake. Lee was executed by firing squad at Mountain Meadows on 23 March 1877.

Hickman's loudest complaint to the end of his book, and no doubt to the end of his life, was the loss of his wives and children. He blamed this on Bishop Archibald Gardner. Hickman was proud of his large family and the fact that he was a great-grandfather at age fifty-six. Most of his children did not finish the eighth grade, and most married in their teens. His grandchildren followed their parents' example. His descendants would inherit little from Hickman besides much regrettable shame.

– 17 –

Wyoming, Death in Peace

After *Brigham's Destroying Angel* appeared on 5 February 1872, while Bill was still in protective custody at Fort Douglas, life was never the same for Hickman. In one quick move he had alienated both Mormons and Gentiles. Everyone was disgusted, Gentiles because he had again escaped the hangman's noose and Mormons because he had vilified their prophet. Hickman's book was available in local bookstores. Its main disclosure was the claim that Brigham Young had ordered Hickman to kill men without a trial because of unbelief.

In 1873 Tom Monaghan, a visitor to Utah, wrote of Bill Hickman: "Today he walks the streets of Salt Lake City shunned like a leper by every respectful man, no one pays attention." Monaghan was a writer for a Kansas magazine and had come to Utah to report on the Mormons. He described the difficulties in the territory after the Gentiles—whom he describes as "fortune hunters, speculators, and thieves"—flooded the area looking for gold in various mining developments. He then gave a blood-curdling account of the "religious fanatic," Bill Hickman, whom he accused of "murdering many in order to secure happiness in the next world."

Over the years the legend of the "Notorious One" would probably have died a quiet death except for frequent, repetitive, and exaggerated tales which were marketed in the East, where readers were hungry for any news about the Mormons and the "Wild West." Hickman came to be known as "Use Him Up Bill."

In his book *The Round Trip*, published in New York in 1879, John Codman described a man he passed on the trail between Cove Fort and Lehi, Utah, as:

> A seedy looking vagabond apparently sixty years of age . . . The expression of his countenance was truly diabolical, and betokened a scoundrel whose society one would intuitively avoid. This was the notorious Bill Hickman, whose residence is in the neighborhood. Why this fiend is permitted to live is a mystery. . . . [H]e walks the streets at night with two revolvers and a belt of cartridges looking for some avenger . . . [and] steeps his damning memory in rum.

This is not to say that Hickman was not feared in Utah. An incident recorded by a young pioneer woman of West Canyon, Utah, in the summer of 1874, showed an image she had of Hickman. She wrote in her journal that

> Then Brother Nathan Willard came running up to the house breathless and screamed for Orpha and Ann to come quickly. He gasped half-crying and told us that a man had killed Nate. We [Zina and her mother], screamed for Orpha and Ann to come back quick. Bill Hickman had just left our place a few minutes before. He heard our shrieks and came back.

As it turned out, Nate was not dead at all but "was covered with the blood of a calf he had just killed and the calf's blood covered rider and horse."

After Hickman's release from the Fort Douglas prison he had returned to Fairfield to rejoin his wife Bernetta. Fairfield was the place he had called home since 1868. Six months after his release he purchased a forty-acre tract about one mile north of town for $500—a large sum of money at the time, especially for Hickman.

In the face of consistent hostility, he became more and more paranoid and reclusive. He wanted to leave Utah for a place of safety, where he would not be recognized or bothered. Whatever plans he made, the complications of his lame hip and the agonizing pain he suffered from the still deeply embedded bullet had to be considered. The old pioneer lawman knew he could not live long. The "typhoid" infection in his leg had reappeared in 1864-65, 1867, and 1870. He described the misery he endured, saying, "I suffered all that a man could suffer and live. I was reduced to skin and bones, lying on my back for months."

Hickman was aware that his wives, children, and grandchildren were ridiculed because of his reputation. Several of the children were raised under other names in small rural communities where their connection to Hickman could not be known.

Hickman began to sell his Fairfield property in March 1873. His last parcel, "Five Mile Spring," which he owned with two others, was sold on 25 May 1880. Possibly within the year he moved to Nephi, into the home of his son-in-law, John Allen, and his daughter, Kitten.

If Hickman received anything for his "confessions," it would not have compensated him for the years of anguish he and his family subsequently suffered. Then came Hickman's final disappointment. Brigham Young died in August 1877, and with him died Hickman's hope that he could be forgiven and welcomed back into the church. Young's death increased Hickman's fear that he would be killed—probably by people who had never known him personally.

To die in peace, Hickman decided to go to Wyoming. He persuaded Bernetta, his first and final wife, to accompany him, along with three of his grown married daughters and their husbands and children. The railroad now stretched from Salt Lake City to Ogden, Utah, and then east through the dry Wyoming plains. But Hickman would only travel by buckboard wagon.

A young grandson recalled the teary farewell as Hickman passed through the town of Nephi where several of his children and grandchildren had settled. "He was lying in the back of the wagon covered with quilts, as he said goodbye to Utah," he said. "He was lying in the wagon because the typhoid sickness had come to his hip again."

The wagon traversed Parley's Canyon, then entered Echo Canyon where Hickman had once defended fellow church members. Hickman had been a great hero in the fall of 1857, twenty-two years before, and a loyal aide to his prophet Brigham Young. The wagon was guided across the Bear River, then the team headed for the new Fort Bridger. It was a journey across mostly flat land, punctuated by narrow ribbons of silver water that meandered through the landscape. They continued across Black's Fork, northeast to the lush rolling plains of Green River, full of memories, toward the Continental Divide on the old Mormon Trail. The old trail was now mostly overgrown with sagebrush.

To settle near Lander would reset the clock back to a happier time, when Hickman and his brother George had had such success in operating their own trading post. The wagon continued north along an old Indian trail, about eight miles, to the headwaters of Baldwin Creek. This would be the last place he would call home. Up in the foothills, sheltered by the protective folds of the Wind River Range, was a place of grassy meadows and craggy mountain peaks, filled with wildlife and punctuated by stands of cottonwood trees and scrub oak.

There were no neighbors, no schools, no stores, no churches, no government officials, no spies. No one lived closer than Lander, and there was not even a proper trail. The high country west of Lander is still accessible only during the four months of summer.

During the late 1870s and early 1880s, Lander, with less than 500 inhabitants, was a gathering place for several apostate Mormon families from Utah. But this was apparently not the reason for Hickman's decision to settle nearby. Hickman had come only to escape, to die, not to complain. If the Grimmitts, the Petersons, the Hudsons, the Rogers, and the Woodrings wanted to voice their hatred of Mormonism at a safe distance from Utah, then let them. Hickman no longer cared.

The four Hickman dugouts were constructed in a line, with about a half-mile between the first and last dugout. Four separate units were needed: one for Bill and Bernetta, one for John and Kitten Allen and their seven children, another for Franklin David Gillespie and his wife Rhoda, and one for Robert Hemphill Gillespie and his wife Phoebe Delilah Hickman. Rhoda and Phoebe were Bill's daughters by Sarah Basford.

The Gillespie brothers had married Hickman sisters at an early age. Phoebe was married a month before she turned sixteen, and arrived on the Baldwin at age nineteen with two small children. She was soon pregnant with a third. Rhoda was married at age sixteen in February 1879. She and her husband came almost as newlyweds to the Baldwin and had no children until 1885, after their return to civilization. Both girls had been raised with the surname "Franks" rather than Hickman, as they were seven and four years old when their mother re-married after Hickman's excommunication in 1868. The Gillespie families had came to Wyoming from Cassia County, Idaho. The fourteen Hickman relatives squatted quietly on the upper Baldwin, paying the five-dollar survey fee required of squatters but none of the Sweetwater County personal property taxes. They would remain there until 1883.

Today the dugout Bill and Bernetta most likely lived in is overgrown with snarls of scrub-oak and lies one-half mile down stream from the larger dugout of Kitten and John Allen. It sits above a steep bank about fifty feet from Baldwin Creek. A narrow footpath goes from the front door of the dugout down the bank through the brush to the stream. The front stone wall faces directly to the east, away from the west wind that blows down from the Wind River Mountains. The dugout construction allowed the families to pass the cruel winters like underground animals. Ventilated only by the door and a space in the dirt roof for escaping smoke, the dugouts were cramped but safe from weather and animals.

As Bill was dying, his family continued to increase. John and Kitten came to Lander with seven of their eventual ten children, ranging in age from one to fourteen years. Two sons, George Elihu Allen and William Adam Allen, were born in the Baldwin Creek dugout. Probably Kitten's mother, Bernetta, and her two sisters-in-law acted as midwives. Robert and Phoebe conceived two children. In December 1881, ten-month-old Robert Jr. died and was buried somewhere in the area.

In August 1882 the oldest daughter of John and Kitten Allen, Loulia Bernetta Allen, married John Perry Smith, a brakeman on the Union Pacific Railroad, in Lander. She was sixteen years old and probably anxious to rejoin civilization, away from the mountain hideout of her parents and grandparents.

A newspaper report printed in the St. Louis *Globe-Democrat* in 1885, two years after Hickman's death, stated that Hickman was "sick for two weeks before he died." The story told in Lander was that he was taken down to the Lander Hotel about three weeks before he passed away to be treated by the doctor from the army post at Fort Washakie, the only doctor in the area. The Lander Hotel in 1883 was a one-storey log cabin. Hickman remained at the hotel until his death on 21 August 1883. The St. Louis *Globe-Democrat* reported that Hickman

> retained consciousness until the last, still a powerful and robust physique. . . . His death was due solely to habits of gross intemperance, whiskey and opium being his sole

articles of diet for days . . . [On his body were] numerous marks of his desperate encounters, his body being seamed [stitched] all over . . . atrocious record and dangerous character made him a man shunned and avoided by all classes here, where he died among the people of the Popo Agie Valley, a *stranger* . . . his kindred gathered up their possessions after his death and took the back trail for Mormondom [the old Indian trail] . . . Among them were the Gillespie brothers, sons-in-law of the dead terror . . . reports say Frank Gillespie is wanted for stealing sheep.

The Gillespie brothers sent news of Hickman's death by telegraph from Lander to the Salt Lake City *Deseret News*, which printed the account on 24 August 1883. The *Tribune* carried the news the following day.

After his death in the Lander Hotel on 21 August, his body was probably taken to the Lander City Cemetery and buried one or two days later. The hot August weather made such speed necessary. There is no record of a religious service preceeding the burial. The Mormons did not have a church in Lander in 1883, and to the people of Lander he was "a stranger."

He was not enough of a stranger, however, for the local citizens to ignore the fact that an outlaw was being buried in the cemetery. The stories in the newspapers of Hickman's body being dug up for reburial seem credible. A new resting place in the country, "a half-mile up the road from the Allen place," satisfied the complaints of the locals and provided the Hickman family with a safe and undisturbed resting place for their notorious loved one.

In the foothills eight miles west of Lander on what is now the Diamond H Ranch, a monument stands, forty feet above a green meadow watered by the turbulent Baldwin Creek. It has been hand-constructed from flat sandstone in the same manner as the front walls of the dugouts close by. This twelve-foot red sandstone edifice rests on a rounded base, which is now partially destroyed. It is the height of a man on horseback and marks the final resting place of William Adams Hickman. The spot was chosen in secrecy by Hickman's family to protect the earthly remains and memorialize him before they abandoned their squatters' claim. Behind the large monument is a smaller man-made stone marker identifying the infant grave and last remains of Hickman's ten-month-old grandson.

On 27 December 1886 Bernetta, aged seventy-four, died in Park City, Utah, among a mostly Gentile population, few of whom cared that her name was Hickman. The Ogden Herald carried the obituary on 31 December: "Bernetta Hickman, a wife of the Notorious Bill Hickman, died at Park City on 27 December 1886. The body has been taken to Nephi for burial, sons George and J. F. Allen and wife accompanied."

Epilogue

Warren Hickman, the seventh child of Bill and Minerva Wade Hickman, was born in 1862 in Salt Lake City and was thus old enough to remember his father before the family broke up in 1868. In 1919 he wrote a short sketch of his father. "The last time I saw my father was at Murray, Utah," Warren wrote. This would have been in 1879 or 1880, when Warren was seventeen or eighteen years old.

> We were camped there. B[isho]p. Hunter came along. I heard him say to my father that he had been misrepresented and greatly wronged. My father said, "Let it go, things will be made right some day." I knew him to be a kind and loving father. People seemed to like him wherever he went. All of his family speak of him in the fondest affectionate way, and all of his charitable deeds, not only at home but abroad.
>
> I read the foregoing to President Lewis Shurtliff and he said he could verify to the truth of all that I had written, having been well acquainted with my father at an early day.

Forty-nine years after Bill Hickman died, his nephew Josiah Edwin Hickman, a professor of history at Utah State University, approached the First Presidency of the Mormon church and asked that Bill Hickman be reinstated into the church posthumously. He recorded his meeting with church leaders in his journal:

> March 22, 1934—I went to Salt Lake again yesterday concerning my uncle William A. Hickman who was excommunicated from the Church about 1868-9 . . . I saw President [Heber J.] Grant to get his sanction to reinstate my uncle. President Grant, A[nthony]. W. Ivins [his counselor],

and [Apostle] George F. Richards all freely gave me permission to do his work, feeling that he had for years done much good for the Church but had fallen away. I am authorized to have all former blessings bestowed on him.

William A. Hickman was rebaptized by proxy into the Church of Jesus Christ of Latter-day Saints on 5 May 1934.

Appendix

William Adams Hickman to His Daughter,
Katharine, 7 January 1872, from Camp Douglas Prison

My Dear Daughter,

You were here some 3 days ago and asked me many questions and desired me for your dear sake as pa's ever affectionate and faithful daughter, to show mercy which disposition in you I highly appreciate, but my daughter let us look at the past, and well consider the present, and then Judge what would naturally be the results of the future.

First my daughter, you know from the days of Missouri when you was a small child you never heard your pa say anything else but Mormonism was true up to the time when you saw me 3 days ago you then heard the same from me that you had heard from the time you was old enough to understand anything, which principles I have ever tryed to maintain and sustain. And after the assassination of that great and good man Joseph Smith the Prophet of God. I took a solem Oath to stand up against all opposition that might come against the Latter-day Saints and specialy for those who might stand at the head of Gods Kingdom. After B. Young took the leadership of the Church, I took the position of sustaining the Church and especially its officials and above all B. Young. I have in time gone by told him so and said to him, I would stand by him and stay with him unto Death, unless he barked me off. This you know I have done. I always obeyed his council and never disobeyed it. I studied his interest and was always on the look out for his welfare and safety, ten times as much as my own. I went and come at his bidding. I spent my own time and used my own means. I made my own living and plenty to support my family in better state than any of my neighbors.

I gave more to the poor and done more for the needy than all my neighbors put together. I swindled no Saint but went outside and gathered in property in abundance.

And never can it be said at any time but what I always done honor to our people in all my business transactions, while hundreds have got wealth in abundance by swindling the poor etc. Now as you know some considerable of this, I need not rehearse it, but probably you do not know that for all my work and privations for B. Young, that I never got a dollar, no not one, neither did he ever make me a present of the worth of a pocket knife, but this was nothing—I had plenty, was able to make plenty so long as I was let alone, but it many times look[ed] strange to me to see those who never raised a finger, receiving favors from him, such as I never would have thought of getting, while to your certain knowledge I never had anything too good for him, neither did I ever have anything that I could not spare for him. You well recollect when we came to Council Bluffs in fall of '47, that I had but two horses. I gave him both of them. We had to live hard, and I worked almost day and night until we started to the valley in the spring of '49, since which time I gave him two number one horses. I herded his cattle in the summer of '50, which would have come to fifty or a hundred dollers. I lost none and charged him nothing. When I returned from California, out of the few hundred dollers I made I gave him fifty, but what of all this. I supposed I was doing Gods service and I took pleasure in it. I took pleasure in walking the streets many a night all alone to see if anything was going on wrong that would have tendency to hurt him. And when in times past there was anything said about what I had done or was doing, never was the time I said a word or I was or had been doing so and so by order of B. Young. I packed everything that was put upon me and kept clear his skirts, and in fact I would at any time had laid down my life for him, but what has been the result, he has ce[a]sed to hear the truth and long since been governed by shallow-brained blowhards, and a vile set of lying City Officials [i.e., Robert T. Burton] and some Bishops such as [Archibald] Gardner, who has stated to us good people as there is in West Jordan that it was no harm to eat my cattle. He who raked [the] Jordan river, on nigger Toms, says so for stolen cattle hides, who was not in the least disposed to believe over 40 of us and repremanded Geo Shields, when on the way down, mob-like, thirty of them, when he said I was not guilty of any such thing. Who has so often said he would *use me up* amidst my every effort to please him, by responding for years to his every call, and after paying him over a thousand dollers [$1,157.31] in tithing and donations. I asked the priviledge of my family to have the benefit of the endowment house, which was refused on the grounds that if he gave me a recommend it would be against his influence. I talked with B. Young about it, he told [me] to go to Bro Kimball. Bro. Kimball told me I must have a recommend from my Bishop. And the consequence was I never got one of my family in[to] the endowment house after his reign commenced. Many of those who my money had helped to bring on had recommends right under our noses.

He was full of deception and lying and to my certain knowledge has got up on Sunday, him and his after eating my cattle and cried, "thief—thief," with all the intimations that could be, I was stealing everything. This went on as you well know untill out of a hundred and fifty head of cattle I had none, while all my neighbors lost none, or but [a] few, what do I think of such a man. He is a villain from the ground up. But yet he is sustained and his damnable deeds tolerated. To sue the language of B. Young when I wanted an investigation of my case, after I had come home 4 years ago last spring, O' bro. Gardner, nows whirling on his heel, when I asked him to hear me as much as to say Kiss his Ass.

You want me to be merciful, that's all good my daughter, but let us look after this man a little further while we are talking about him. Was not my house watched 4 years ago last spring, by his dirty thieves and his armed villains slipping into my house with kocked guns, and pistols in hand. Yes, I seen them and through the mercy of God I escaped, and to continue what was the condition of things in the fall following. Why that low-bred dog Sam Bateman, with ten men watched me day and night for weeks, and twice while laying in the brush, seen them with pistols in hand step into my tent after midnight. Finally they set the time to make a finish of me, but thanks be to my God I understood it all, and left. And poor Sam made great lamentation that he had lost 3 weeks watching me and now I had got away after all. Maybe he will deny this, but my proof is on hand. Who ordered this. O pa you must be merciful. Yes, daughter that's right, but to go on, who sent Bazel Hampton after me? Who followed me with two others to deep creek with the story in their mouths that I had killed a Gentile close to the city, and robed him of ten thousand dollers. Yes, who sent him out of the City. Well you guess. I know, maybe he would deny it. My proofs are in Bingham Cannon, and more than one. O yes, pa be merciful. May I ask you who has managed everything in this country. Well you know. I will tell you. I have told to him most of these things, and for an answer I think I just about got a grunt or nothing more in substance. But to continue on with this trip, while I am at it. You know I was sick while gone, yes, I lay 4 months [or] more a scelition [skeleton] among strangers. Well, I wrote home to B. Young stating facts as I have to you, and the answer was "The wicked fleeth when no man persueth."

O the falsehood and hipocracy my God, my God. Where has right and truth fled to, probably to those police, together with the Probate Court. Old [Elias] Smith at their head, who when I had detected and found those thieves in possession of some 5 or 6 thousand dollers worth of stolen goods, they would take the reward, my earnings and set the burglars to swear against me in order to cover their rascallity, and kept them at it 3 months. Although they did not make their point, the thieves done so well they got off with a promise of a pay something some time. Yes, you know this.

What did they try to do with me. Imprison, and I gave a hundred and eighteen thousand dollers bail. Who winked at this and would not hear a word. Well, now my daughter I am arrested on several charges, and many think it a great crime in me that I am not willing to pack all the charges that are on me, submit and say nothing. Well, had I had the treatment that a common dog should have had, I would have done it unto death. Now suppose I had my family together, which was the best governed family in Utah, could I not in all good faith have left them, went to Mexico and let everything be laid on me. I would have taken pleasure even in death for my friends, but they say I am a traitor. Who is the traitor. When last fall I was accused of killing a desperado Spaniard who had taken my wife while I was run off by those murderers four years ago, and he the villain making his brags how he intended to seduce my daughter—your sister. The *Deseret News*, the main Mormon organ under the control and dictation of the leading men, says that well-known desperado has killed a Spaniard, a good man, and wounded a frenchman. He who has so often through his cunning escaped the ends of justice. They hoped he would be caught and the ends of the law fully awarded to him, and again what did they say when I was arrested, and brought here? They hooted again and pated the marshall for the good thing he had done. Do you suppose for one moment that I am able to fight the Gentiles with the Mormon aid that was on hand, and offering to help them wishing writs to arreast me etc. Thats a biger fight than I can make. I am thrown off. Have been refused an investigation [a line is missing due to a fold in the letter] . . . have had it I could have made twenty thousand dollars out of it in one year, but no I could not get it. It was left for others and the desert has no turnpike yet. If I asked a favour that there was money in that no one had any claim in, I could not get it. Well, you know how I have been treated. As regards the breaking up of my family. That good and great family have through council been scattered, some one way and some another. And when I did not stay at home to be killed, I was cut off of the Church because I fled to save my life, and Geo A. Smith sit by, who I have done so many favors, and never said a word. Well, this was one of the made up cases and thoroughly ordered all the way down. Well, upon the whole what have I got to live for. First my religion, and second my posterity and friends. I also live to help gods people and good men but Gods would be the rascals, traitors, robbers, assasins and seekers of my distruction.

    I am under no obligation to let those whose lies have been believed and truth crowded out, take care of those who have believed them, and I for one want to see if God Almighty will assist and sustain a set of scoundrels and have the innocent destroyed. My prayer is, Thy will be done O father of heaven and earth and not mine. I have done nothing through fear or with the expectation of reward. The many and damnable abuses I have received has caused the charms of life not to be longer desirable, but I have faith to believe I will yet, according to the prophecies placed upon me, see Zion established and flourish and my posterity gathered to rejoice. The lord will bring it about in his own way, while all corruption will go to its own place.

    The past I have scarcely lived through as for the present I know there is no honour. While you would ask mercy for certain ones they to my certain knowledge are seeking any way to destroy me even up to this day. The full ends of the future I know not, but one thing I do know, God Almighty rules and reigns, and its him I thank for all my existance. In spite of all that men can do.

I have since I came here had to make statements. I have written a rough book [*Brigham's Destroying Angel*] but no more rough than true. I knew what I had to contend against, but yet although no favour would be shewn me, or if any, a mere blind to answer their own ends.

I will be merciful. I have and always had influence. I have it still in some respects. I will use it according to your request, but I must do it in my own way and if things move quietly through in a right manner I can. I will. Yes, daughter I will, but if I am compelled I have only begun to withstand a few things that have come up.

from your affectionate father
Wm. A. Hickman

[A certified copy of the above letter, dated 29 January 1872, is located in the archives of the Historical Department, Church of Jesus Christ of Latter-day Saints, Salt Lake City, Utah. The location of the original, if it still survives, is unknown.]

William Adams Hickman, 1815-83 (courtesy Utah State Historical Society).

Minerva Wade Hickman, third plural wife of Bill Hickman (courtesy the author).

Brigham Young, second president of the Church of Jesus Christ of Latter-day Saints and friend of Bill Hickman until 1863 (courtesy Utah State Historical Society).

Orson Hyde, Mormon apostle who defended Bill Hickman's stealing from Gentiles at Winter Quarters, telling him to "go and sin no more" (courtesy of Utah State Historical Society).

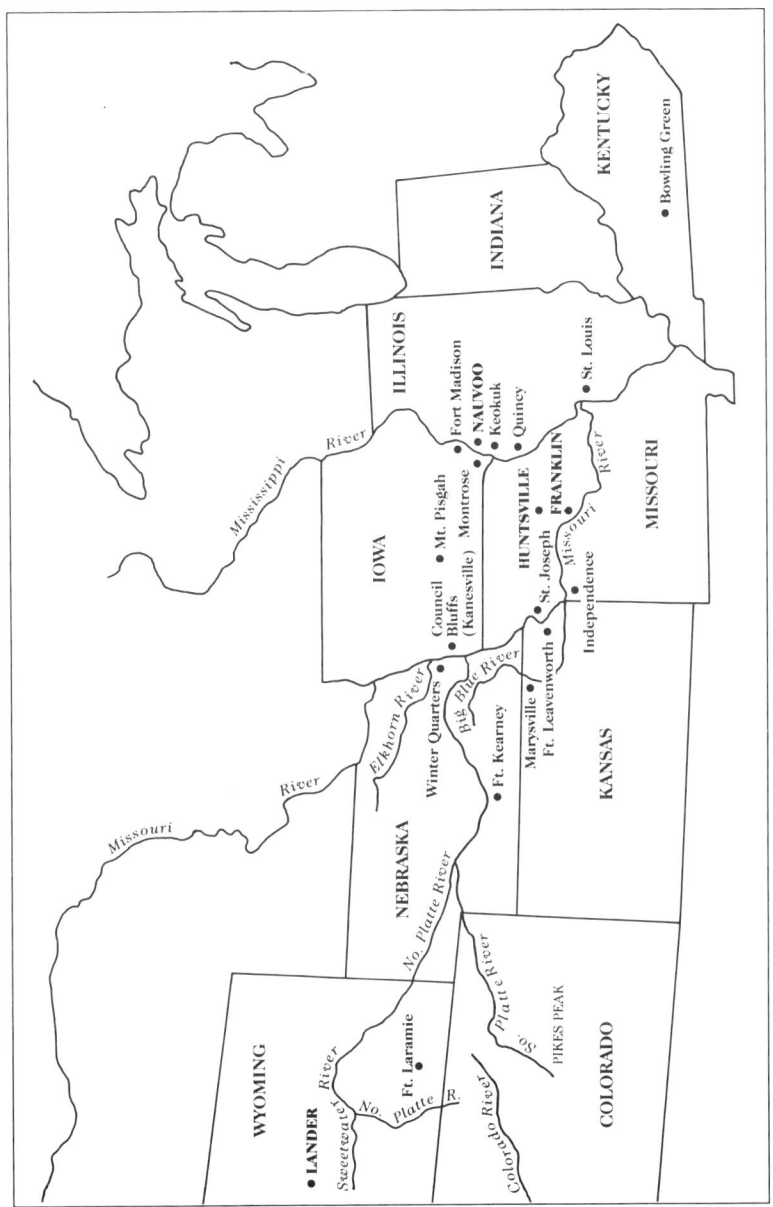

Bill Hickman's West, 1815-49. Born 10 miles south of Bowling Green (KY), he was raised in Franklin (MO), educated in Huntsville (MO), and fought in the Battle of Nauvoo (IL).

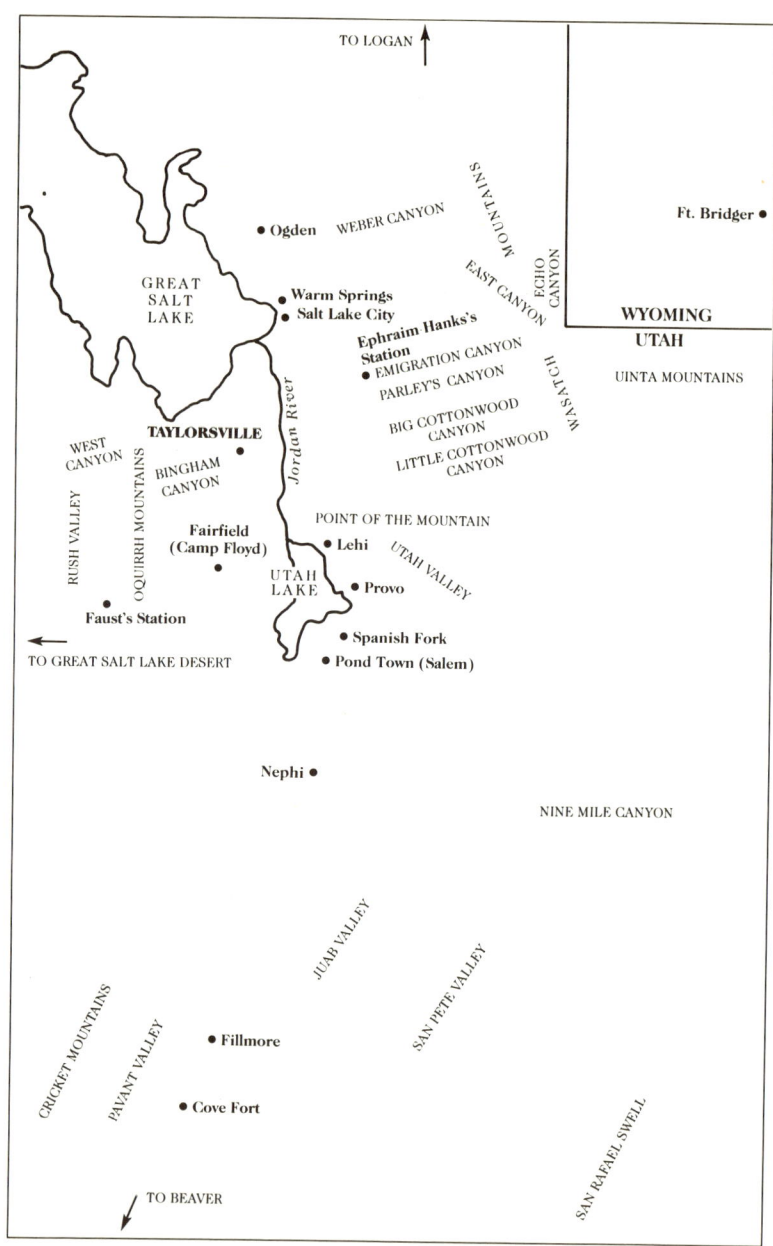

The Salt Lake Valley Region, 1849-72. Hickman settled in Taylorsville, battled Indians in Provo and Ogden, and was crippled in 1859 in a gun fight in Salt Lake City.

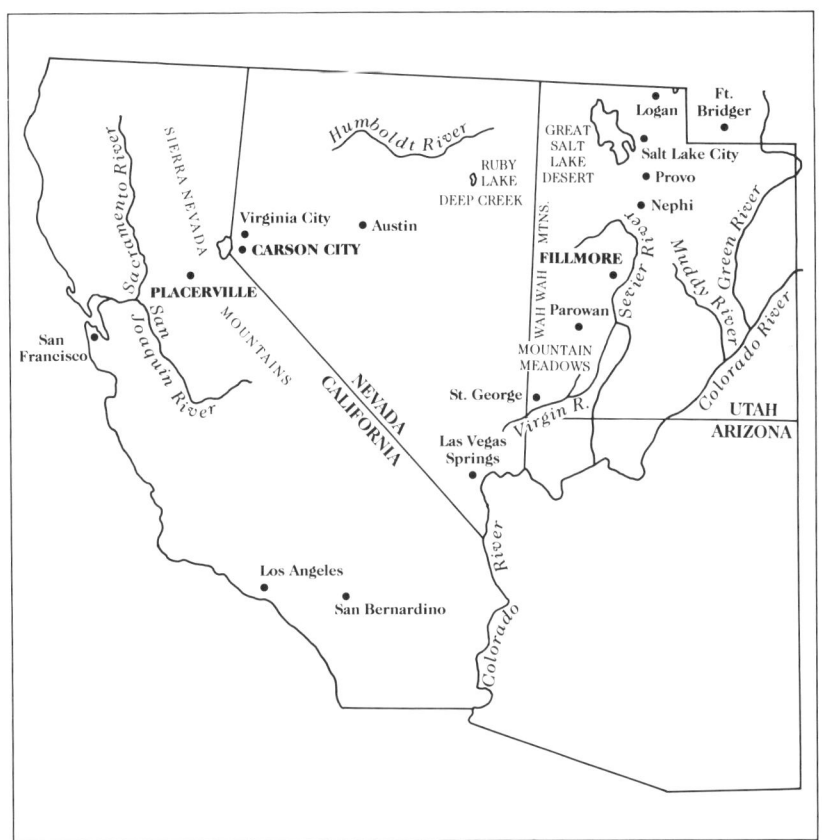

The Rocky Mountain West and Nevada/California mining fields where Bill Hickman prospected for gold and took part in cattle drives.

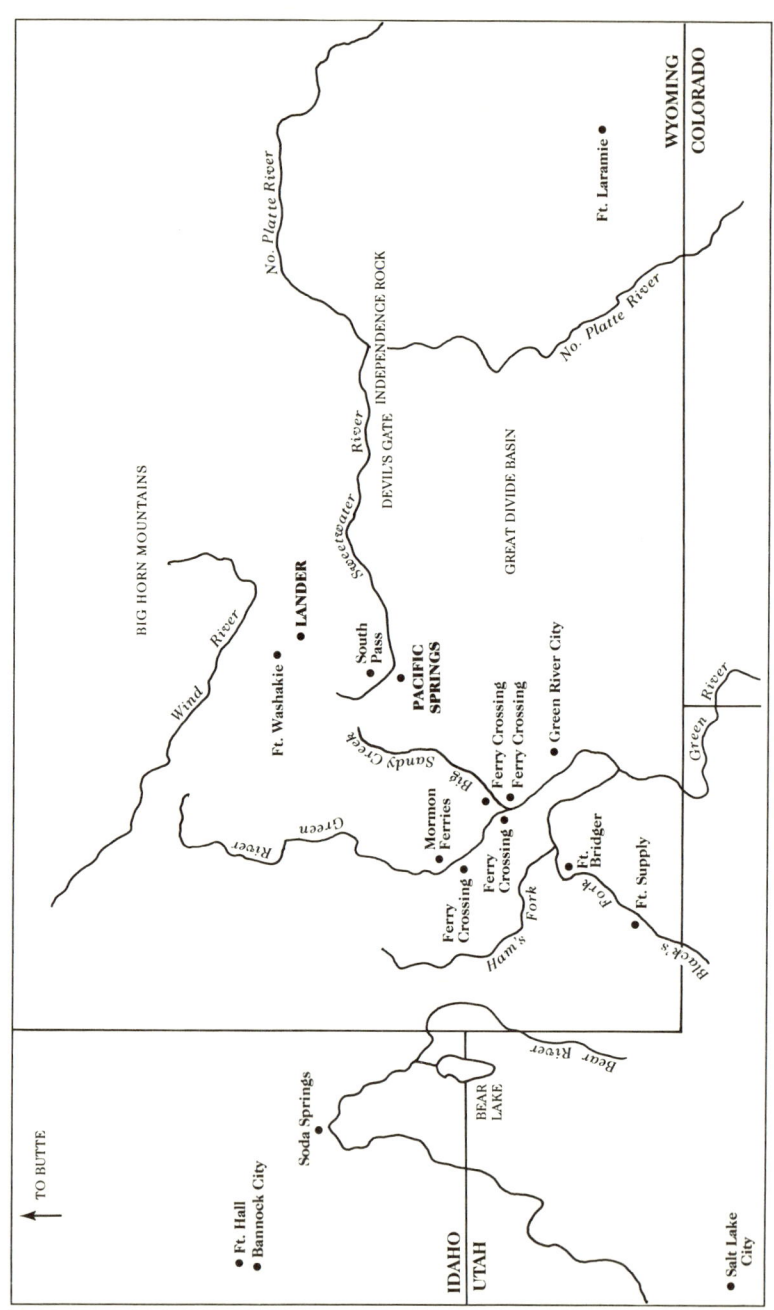

The Green River Country and Wyoming Wilderness. Hickman operated ferries on the Green River and was a deputy marshall and county sheriff. In 1883 he died and was buried in Lander, Wyoming.

Washakie, chief of the Shoshone for over forty years with whom Bill Hickman negotiated a peace settlement at Ogden in 1854 and at Fort Bridger in 1856 (courtesy Utah State Historical Society).

Artist's conception of Fort Bridger in 1855 when Bill Hickman purchased it for the Mormon church (courtesy Utah State Historical Society).

James Bridger, mountain man and founder of Fort Bridger until 1855 (courtesy Utah State Historical Society).

Louis Vasquez, partner of James Bridger at Fort Bridger (courtesy Utah State Historical Society).

Orrin Porter Rockwell, Mormon frontiersman, lawman, scout, and rival of Bill Hickman during the 1860s (courtesy Utah State Historical Society).

Alfred Cumming, second Utah territorial governor, accompanied Albert Sidney Johnston during the Utah Expedition, 1857-58 (courtesy Utah State Historical Society).

Albert Sidney Johnston, commander of the federal troops sent to Utah to subdue Mormon rebellion (courtesy Utah State Historical Society).

Camp Floyd, which members of the Utah Expedition established (courtesy Utah State Historical Society).

Townsend Hotel, downtown Salt Lake City, where Bill Hickman recuperated after having been critically shot and left for dead (courtesy Utah State Historical Society).

John W. Dawson served as Utah territorial governor for only twenty-one days before dying from a beating he received from Bill Hickman's gang in 1861 (courtesy Utah State Historical Society).

Ephraim K. Hanks, purported "Danite" at whose waystation east of Salt Lake City Bill Hickman's gang beat Governor Dawson (courtesy Utah State Historical Society).

Patrick Edward Connor, commander of the California Volunteers in Utah during the Civil War and founder of Fort Douglas in 1862 (courtesy Utah State Historical Society).

Utah miners of 1863—Bill Hickman is second from the left on the back row (Salt Lake Tribune photograph).

Fort Douglas guardhouse (right center), where Bill Hickman was held in protective custody in 1871-72 (courtesy Utah State Historical Society).

The Lander, Wyoming, Hotel, where Bill Hickman reportedly died in 1883 (courtesy the author).

Bibliography

Abbott, Delila. *Days of Our Fathers*. Salt Lake City: D. M. Abbott, 1981.

Allen, James B., and Glen M. Leonard. *The Story of the Latter-day Saints*. Salt Lake City: Deseret Book, 1976.

Alter, J. Cecil, ed. "The Utah War, Journal of Albert Tracy 1858 to 1860." *Utah State Historical Quarterly* 13 (1945): 1-118.

An Act of the Legislative Assembly, Territory of Utah, 27 Dec. 1855, Utah State Archives.

Anderson, Nelson. *Desert Saints*. Chicago: University of Chicago Press, 1942.

Armstrong, Perry A. *The Sauks and the Black Hawk War*. Springfield, IL, 1887.

Arrington, Leonard J. *Great Basin Kingdom: An Economic History of the Latter-day Saints, 1830-1900*. Lincoln: University of Nebraska Press, 1966.

——, and Hope A. Hilton. "Setting the Record Straight." Task Papers in LDS History, Aug. 1979, No. 28. Library/Archives, Historical Department, Church of Jesus Christ of Latter-day Saints, Salt Lake City, Utah; hereafter, LDS church archives.

Austin, Emily M. *Mormonism; or Life Among the Mormons*. Madison, WI, 1882.

Banal, Eugene. *Frontier Life in the Army, 1854-1861*. Glendale, CA: Arthur H. Clark Co., 1932.

Bancroft, Hubert Howe. *History of Utah*. San Francisco, 1890.

Bank, John. "A Document History of the Morrisites." M.A. thesis, University of Utah, 1908.

Baskin, R. N. *Reminiscences of Early Utah*. Salt Lake City, 1914.

Bayard, Samuel J. *The Life of George Dashrell Bayard*. New York, 1874.

Beadle, J. H., ed. *Brigham's Destroying Angel: Being the Life, Confessions, and Startling Disclosures of the Notorious, Bill Hickman*. New York City, 1872.

————. *Life in Utah*. Toronto, 1872.

Bean, George W. *Autobiography*. Utah Printing Co., 1945.

Bennett, Richard E. *Mormons at the Missouri, 1846-1852*. Norman: University of Oklahoma Press, 1987.

Bennion, John. Diary, 1850-75. Special Collections, Harold B. Lee Library, Brigham Young University, Provo, Utah.

Birney, Hoffman. *Zealots of Zion*. Philadelphia, 1931.

Bowles, Samuel. *Across the Continent*. New York, 1868.

Brigham Young's "Proclamation." 5 Aug. 1857. Beinecke Library, Yale University.

Brodie, Fawn M. *No Man Knows My History*. New York: Alfred A. Knopf, 1945.

Brooks, Juanita, and Robert Glass Cleland, eds. *A Mormon Chronicle: The Diaries of John D. Lee*. 2 vols. Salt Lake City: University of Utah Press, 1983.

Brooks, Juanita, ed. *Hosea Stout, On the Mormon Frontier*. 2 vols. Salt Lake City: University of Utah Press, 1964.

————. *Mountain Meadows Massacre*. Stanford: Stanford University Press, 1962.

Brown, James S. *Giant of the Lord*. Salt Lake City: Bookcraft, 1960.

————. *Life of a Pioneer*. Salt Lake City: George Q. Cannon and Sons Co., 1900.

Burton, Richard F. *The City of the Saints*. Edited by Fawn M. Brodie. New York: Alfred A. Knopf, 1963.

Campbell, Eugene. *Establishing Zion: The Mormon Church in the American West, 1847-1869*. Salt Lake City: Signature Books, 1988.

Campbell, Robert Lang. Journal. Special Collections, Brigham Young University.

Carson, John. "Use Him Up Bill." *True West Magazine* 2 (May-June 1964): 16-23.

Carter, Kate B., ed. *Our Pioneer Heritage*. Vols. 8, 9, and 15. Salt Lake City: Daughters of the Utah Pioneers.

Church Office Journal. 1857, 1858, and 1860. LDS church archives.

Clark, William, "A Trip Across the Plains in 1857." *Iowa Journal of History and Politics* 20 (April 1922): 163-223.

Coates, Lawrence G. "Brigham Young and Mormon Indian Policies: The Formative Period 1836-1851." *Brigham Young University Studies* 18 (Spring 1978): 432-38.

Codman, John. *The Round Trip, By Way of Panama Through California, Oregon, Utah, Idaho, and Colorado*. New York, 1879.

Cowley, Matthias F., ed. *Wilford Woodrff*. Salt Lake City: Deseret Book, 1909.

Cradlebaugh, John. *Inside Mormonism*. Compiled by George L. Faull. Joplin, MO: College Press, 1969.

Creer, Leland Hargrove. *Utah and the Nation*. Seattle: University of Washington Press, 1929.

Davies, J. Kenneth. *Mormon Gold: The Story of California's Mormon Argonauts*. Salt Lake City: Olympus Publishing Company, 1984.

Dewey, Richard Lloyd. *Porter Rockwell: The Definitive Biography*. New York: Paramount Books, 1986.

Diary of Lorenzo Brown, 1823-1900. Lethro Heritage Press: 198?.

"Early Church Blessings." LDS church archives.

"Early History of Carson Valley." Dictated 27 April 1881. Pioneer Memories. Bancroft Library.

Ellison, Robert S. *Fort Bridger, Wyoming, a Brief History*. Casper, WY, 1931.

Erikson, Joan. "William Adams Hickman, An Enigma in Mormon History." LDS church archives.

Fabian, Harold P. "Camp Floyd." Army of Utah Records, National Archives, Washington, D.C.

Ferris, Benjamin G. *Utah and the Mormons, The History, Government, Doctrines, Customs, and Prospects of the*

Latter-day Saints. New York, 1854.

Fitch, Thomas. "Utah Constitutional Convention, 20 February 1872." LDS church archives.

Flanders, Robert Bruce. *Nauvoo, Kingdom on the Mississippi.* Urbana: University of Illinois Press, 1965. Fox, William. "Patrick Edward Connor." M.A. thesis, Brigham Young University, 1966.

Furniss, Norman F. *The Mormon Conflict.* New Haven: Yale University Press: New Haven, 1960.

Gates, Susa Young. *John Stevens' Courtship, a Story of the Echo Canyon War.* Salt Lake City, 1909.

Godfrey, Audrey M. "Housewives, Hussies, and Heroines, or the Women of Johnston's Army." *Utah Historical Quarterly* 54 (Spring 1986): 157-78.

Gove, Jesse A. *The Utah Expedition 1857-1858, Letters of Capt. Jesse A. Gove.* Concord, NH: Historical Society, 1928.

Gowans, Fred R. "Fort Bridger and the Mormons." *Utah Historical Quarterly* 42 (Winter 1974): 50-67.

―――, and Eugene E. Campbell. *Fort Bridger, Island in the Wilderness.* Provo, UT: Brigham Young University Press, 1975.

Gray, John S. "The Salt Lake Hockaday Mail: Part I." *Annals of Wyoming* 56 (Fall 1984): 12-19.

―――. "The Salt Lake Hockaday Mail: Part II." *Annals of Wyoming* 57 (Spring 1985): 2-11.

Greer, Deon C. *Atlas of Utah.* Provo, UT: Brigham Young University Press, 1981.

Hamilton, Henry S. *Reminiscence of a Veteran.* Concord, NH, 1897.

Hammond, William Wallace. "Autobiography," 1939. Special Collections, Brigham Young University.

Harding, Neil Dickson. "William Adams Hickman, Was He the Man We Think He Is?" Special Collections, Brigham Young University.

Harstad, Peter. "The Lander Trail." *Idaho Yesterdays* 12 (Fall 1968): 14-28.

Hebard, Grace R. *Washakie.* Cleveland: Arthur H. Clark Co., 1930.

Hickman, Minerva Wade. "My Story." Special Collections, Brigham Young University.
Hickman, Minerva Wade. Notebook. In author's possession.
Hickman, Warren Edwin. *An Echo from the Past*. Denver, CO, 1914.
Hickman, Warren W. "Tribute to Wm. A. Hickman." In *Heart Throbs of the West* 6. Salt Lake City: Daughters of the Utah Pioneers, 1945, 428-31.
Hickman, William Adams. Letter to Minerva Wade Hickman, 8 Feb. 1868. Special Collections, Brigham Young University.
Hickman, William Adams. Letters to Brigham Young (13 July 1854, 23 Aug. 1857, Dec. 1859, Jan. 1860, 10 Oct. 1861, 25 June 1862, 30 Dec. 1862, 14 Jan. 1864, 7 Jan. 1865, 25 April 1866, 15 Aug. 1868). LDS church archives.
Hill, Donna. *Joseph Smith: The First Mormon*. Salt Lake City: Signature Books, 1977.
Hilton, Hope A. "William Adams Hickman, Mormon Mountain Man." Unpublished manuscript, 1978, 1983.
——————. "Edwin and Ellender Hickman, Some Progenitors, and Descendants, of Virginia, North Carolina, Kentucky, Missouri, and Utah." Unpublished manuscript, 1967, 1969, 1978.
History of Lee County, Iowa. Chicago, 1879.
Hogan, Mervin B. "James B. McKean." Research Lodge of Utah Masonic Temple, 1975.
Hughes, Delila Gardner. *The Life of Archibald Gardner*. Archibald Gardner Family Genealogical Association, 1939.
Hyde, John, Jr. *Mormonism*. New York, 1857.
Hyde, Orson. Letter to Brigham Young, 25 April 1850. LDS church archives.
Jennings, N. M. "Carson Valley." *Nevada Historical Papers* 1 (1913-16): 178-83.
Johnston, Albert S. Correspondence to the Officers of the Utah Expedition, 1857-58. War Records, National Archives.
——————. Correspondence. Headquarters Department of Utah, Camp Floyd, Utah Territory, National Archives.
Jones, Daniel W. *Forty Years Among the Indians*. Salt Lake City, 1890.

Jordan Ward Records. LDS church archives.

Kenney, Scott G., ed. *Wilford Woodruff's Journal.* 9 vols. Salt Lake City: Signature Books, 1983-85.

Kimball, Heber C. Diary. LDS church archives.

King, Terral F. *The Pony Express Rides Again.* Reprint; Fall 1965, 1-3.

Larson, T. A. *History of Wyoming.* Lincoln: University of Nebraska Press, 1965.

Laub, George. Journal. Special Collections, Brigham Young University.

Lee, John D. *Mormonism Unveiled or the Life & Confessions of John D. Lee.* St. Louis, 1878.

Linn, William Alexander. *The Story of the Mormons, From the Date of Their Origins to the Year 1901.* New York: Russell and Russell, Inc., 1963.

Little, H. *Mail Service Across the Plains.* Salt Lake City, 1884.

Martineau, James Henry. Unpublished manuscript dated 23 July 1907. Iron Military District, National Archives.

McAllister, John D. Autobiography and Diary, 1847-60. Special Collections, Brigham Young University.

McIntosh, William. Diary. Special Collections, Brigham Young University.

Merritt, Frank Clinton. *The History of Alameda County, California.* Vol. 2. S.J. Clarke Publishing Co., 1928.

Monaghan, Tom. "Utah and the Mormons." *Kansas Magazine* 4 (Sept., 1873): 281-87.

Mormoniad. Boston, 1858.

Murphy, J. W. *Outlaws of the Fox River Country.* Hannibal, MO, 1882.

"Narrative of Franklin Dewey Richards." Bancroft Library.

Neff, Andrew Love. *History of Utah, 1847-1869.* Edited and annotated by Leland Hargrave Greer. Salt Lake City: Deseret News Press, 1940.

Nelson, Robert C. *History of Lee County.* Vol. 1. Chicago: Clark Publishing, 1914.

Newell, Linda King, and Valeen Tippetts Avery. *Mormon Enigma.* New York: Doubleday and Co., 1984.

Norman, Mary Baily S. Letter to Ina Coolbirth, 24 April 1908. Archives, Reorganized Church of Jesus Christ of Latter Day Saints, Independence, MO.

O'Neil, Hugh F., ed. "Incidents in Utah History." Bancroft Library.

Perkins, J. R. *Mormon Battalion*. Council Bluffs, IO, 1932.

———. *Yesterday, Today and Tomorrow, Council Bluffs, Pottawattomi County, Iowa, 1856-1956*. Council Bluffs, IA, 1956.

Pitkin, George Orin. "Mormon Diaries." Vol 3. Special Collections, Brigham Young University.

Probate Court Records, Davis County, Salt Lake County, Green River County, Shambip County, Tooele County. Utah State Archives.

"Profiles of William A. Hickman." Unpublished manuscript compiled by Hickman Family Organization, 1980.

Rae, W. F. *Westward By Rail, The New Route to the East*. New York, 1871.

Reese, John. "Mormon Station." *Nevada Historical Papers* 1 (1913-16): 186-90.

Reid, J. M. *Sketches and Anecdotes of the Old Settlers and New Comers, the Mormon Bandites and Danite Band*. Keokuk, IO, 1876.

Richards, Franklin Dewey. "Letters and Notes on Utah History." Bancroft Library.

Richards, W. *Old Trail Guide, Mormon Way-Bill to the Gold Mines from the Pacific Springs, North and Southern Mountains*. Salt Lake City, 1851.

Richardson, Albert D. *Beyond the Mississippi*. New York, 1867.

Richman, Irving B. *John Brown Among the Quakers and Other Sketches*. Des Moines, IA, 1894.

Roberts, B. H. *A Comprehensive History of the Church of Jesus Christ of Latter-day Saints, Century I*. 6 vols. Salt Lake City: Deseret New Press, 1930.

Rockwood, Albert Perry. "A Concise History of the Utah Penitentiary, Its Inmates and Officers 1855 to 1878." Bancroft Library.

Rogan, Francis Edward. "Patrick Edward Connor, An Army

Officer in Utah, 1862-1866." M.A. thesis, University of Utah, 1952.

Rogers, Fred B. *Soldiers of the Overland, The Life of Patrick Connor.* San Francisco: Grabhorn Press, 1938.

Ross, James. *From Wisconsin to California and Return.* Madison, WI, 1869.

Schindler, Harold. *Orrin Porter Rockwell, Man of God, Son of Thunder.* Salt Lake City: University of Utah Press, 1966.

Sweetwater County Land and Tax Records, 1880-83. County Courthouse, Green River, WY.

Sketches & Anecdotes of Old Settlers Association of Lee County, Iowa. Keokuk, IA, 1877.

Skidmore, Rex A. "Penology in Early Utah." *Humanities Review* (April 1948).

Smith, Joseph, et al. *History of the Church of Jesus Christ of Latter-day Saints, 1830-1848.* 7 vols. Salt Lake City: Deseret Book Co., 1956. Smith, Joseph, III. "Memoirs." RLDS church archives.

Smith, Mary Ettie V. *Fifteen Years Among the Mormons.* Chicago, 1876.

Stegner, Wallace. *The Gathering of Zion, The Story of the Mormon Trail.* New York: McGraw Hill, 1964.

Stenhouse, T. B. H. *The Rocky Mountain Saints.* New York, 1873.

Stone, Wilbur Fish, ed. *The History of Colorado.* Chicago: S. J. Clarke Publishing Co., 1918.

Story of a Trail. San Pedro, Los Angeles, and Salt Lake Railroad Company, 1905.

Stratton, Fred D., Jr. "Early History of South Pass City, Wyoming, and How Women First Received the Right to Vote and Hold Public Office." Lander, WY.

Taylor, John. "Reminiscences." Bancroft Library.

Tullidge, Edward W. *History of Salt Lake City.* Salt Lake City, 1886.

Tuttle, Newton. "Accounts and Diary, 1852-1860," 128-41. Utah State Historical Society.

Utah Expedition, Containing a General Account of the Mormon Campaign, by a Wagon Master of the Expedition. Cincinnati, OH, 1858.

Van Orden, Richard Dale. "A History of the Utah State Prison." Special Collections, Marriott Library, University of Utah Library, Salt Lake City.

Vanderhoff, Lerona Minerva Hickman. "Letter to the Daughters of the Utah Pioneers." In *An Enduring Legacy* 3. Salt Lake City: Daughters of the Utah Pioneers, 1980, 41-49.

Walker, Charles L. Diary. Special Collections, Brigham Young University.

Whitcomb, Elias W. "Reminiscences of a Pioneer." *Annals of Wyoming* 57 (Fall 1985): 21-32.

Whitney, Orson F. *History of Utah*. 4 vols. Salt lake City, 1893.

William Clayton's Journal. Salt Lake City: Clayton Family Association, 1921.

Young, Brigham. Letters to William Adams Hickman (7 Jan. 1865, 14 June 1867, 28 Aug. 1868). LDS church archives.

Index

A

Abrams, Levi, 48, 54
Adair County (MO), 64
Adams County (IL), 9, 11
Adams, Elizabeth. *See* Hickman, Elizabeth
adultery, 125
Aiken Gang (also Aiken, John; Aiken, Thomas), 69, 70, 71
Alexander, Colonel, 74, 75, 76
Allen, George Elihu, 133
Allen, John F., 131, 132, 133, 134, 135
Allen, Loulia Bernetta, 133
Allen, Captain, 16
Allen, William Adams, 133
Alvaton (KY), 3
American Fur Co., 55
Anderson, Captain, 18
Anderson, Kirk, 84
Andrus, Brother, 53
Angel, Truman O., 31
Appleby, I., 43, 44, 45, 47
Armstrong, Mr., 57
Arnold, Josiah, 85, 86, 108
Ash Hollow, 60
Austin (NV), 117
Avenging Angels, 40

B

Babbitt, Almon W., 20, 25
Bad Axe Battle, 6
Baker's Ferry, 66
Baltimore (MD), 53
Banal, Eugene, 73
Bancroft, Hubert H., 28
Banks, Joseph, 105
Bannock City (ID), 100, 107
baptism, 6-7, 115
Barney, Alvira, 127
Barren River (KY), 3
Basford, Sarah. *See* Hickman, Sarah Basford
Baskin, R. N., 125, 127
Bateman, Samuel, 100
Battle Creek Hills (UT), 111
Beadle, James H., 8, 127
Bean, George W., 28, 47
Bear River (UT), 74, 131
Beaver City (UT), 128
Bennion, John, 28, 36, 56, 61, 71, 74, 80, 86, 95, 96, 97, 99, 100
Bennion, Samuel, 28, 30, 53
Bent County (CO), 37, 88
Big Blue River, 60
Big Elk, 29, 37
Big Field, 32, 33
Big Mountain (UT), 99
Bigler, J. G., 23
Bigler, John H., 45
Bingham Canyon mines, 99, 109, 117
Black Hawk War, 6, 24
Black, John, 62
Black's Creek (WY), 38, 79
Black's Fork, 131
Blair, Mr., 86
Boggs, Lilburn W., 7
Boonesville (MO), 64
Bowling Green (KY), 2
Boyd, George A., 31, 43, 53, 62
Bridger, Jim, 29, 32, 37, 38, 39, 40, 48, 52
Brigham City (UT), 7
Brown, James S., 40, 47, 48, 51
Brown, Lorenzo, 78, 89
Brown Sal, 100
Buchanan, James, 60, 64, 79, 80

Bullock, Isaac, 42, 51, 56
Bullock, Miss, 43
Bullock, Thomas, 31
Bunton, Samuel, 107, 108
Burckhardt, Bernetta. *See* Hickman, Bernetta
Burckhardt, George, 5
Burckhardt, Greenlief, 7
Burton, Judge, 48
Burton, Sir Richard, 8, 12, 29
Burton, Robert T., 31, 40, 79, 105, 111, 112
Butcher, Katharine Hickman, 89, 127
Butcher, Samuel Monroe, 87, 89, 90, 91, 108, 113
Butte (MT), 124
Byington, Hyrum Elliott, 98
BYX Company, 59, 61, 63, 64, 65

C

California, 30, 31, 33, 36, 37, 84, 85, 86, 100, 103, 104, 105, 110
Camp of Death, 79
Campbell, James, 61
Camp Floyd, 83, 84, 85, 92, 98, 99, 100, 103, 108
Camp Floyd Mining District, 121
Carterville (NE), 24
Carthage Jail, 11
Carrington, Albert, 48, 79, 86, 125
Carson City (NV), 68, 118, 119
Case, Martha Diantha. *See* Hickman, Diana Case
Cassia County (ID), 132
cavalry, 75, 104, 111
Cedar County (UT), 88
Chapman, John, 69, 70
Chihauhau (Mexico), 38
Clark, William, 74
Clauson, Moroni, 87, 91, 100, 101
Clayton, William, 18
Codman, John, 130
coffee, 78
Collett, Sylvanus, 70, 71
Colorado, 88, 103, 104
Connor, Patrick, 103, 104, 105, 109, 110, 111, 114, 115, 116, 118, 119, 120
Cook, Colonel, 67, 68, 98
Cornwall, Alexander, 24, 27
Council Bluffs. *See* Winter Quarters
Council of Fifty, 12
counterfeiters, 20
Cove Fort, 130
Cradlebaugh, Judge, 85
Crosbey, Captain, 41
Crow, Leonard H., 11

Culpeper County (VA), 2, 3
Cumberland Gap, 2
Cumming, Alfred, 67, 79, 80, 99
Cumming, Elizabeth, 80
Cummings, James W., 53
Cutler, Orson, 100
Culter's Park (NE), 19

D

Daily Gate City (IA), 126
Dalton, Simon, 127
Dame, Colonel, 21, 68
Dame, William, 72
Danites. *See* Hickman, William Adams
Dauganser, Louis, 87, 112
Davies, Colonel, 99
Dawson, John M., 99, 100
Decker, Charles F., 60
Deep Creek (NV), 117
Dempsey, Bob, 103
Deshand, Mr., 74
Destroying Angels. *See* Hickman, William Adams
detective, 114
Devil's Gate, 60, 63
Diamond H Ranch (WY), 134
Douglas, Stephen A., 104
dragoons, 67, 68
Drake, Horace, 22
Drown, C. M., 85, 86, 108
Drummond, W. W., 53, 54, 64

E

East Canyon (UT), 43, 61, 71
Echo Canyon (UT), 32, 77, 78, 87, 131
Eckles, Chief Justice, 79, 84, 92
Elkhorn River (IA), 20
Emery, George B., 128
Endowment House, 44, 52, 85
England, 2
Erchad, "Colonel," 69, 70
Ethier, Anthony, 111
Extermination Order, 7

F

Fairfield (UT), 80
Farmersville (NY), 21
Farmington (UT), 86
Faust's Station (UT), 100
fast day, 59
Felt, Nathaniel A., 31
Ferguson, James, 39, 40, 41, 79

INDEX 157

Ferries, Green River. *See* Hickman, William Adams
Fillmore (UT), 52, 53, 54
Five Mile Spring (UT), 131
Flack, John, 78, 87, 90, 91, 125
Fort Bridger, 69, 71, 72, 73, 74, 75, 77, 79, 83, 99, 131
Fort Douglas, 110, 127, 129, 130
Fort Hall, 98
Fort Laramie, 40, 60, 63, 74
Fort Leavenworth, 67, 68, 71, 74, 75
Fort Madison, 10
Fort Supply, 42, 43, 52, 63, 73
Fort Washakie, 133
Fontenelle Creek, 75
Frances, William, 118
Franklin (MO), 4
Franks, John, 119, 132
Fremont, John C., 38
Fremont Peak (WY), 51
Frontier Guardian, 19, 23
Frost, Huldah, 14

G

Gallard (IO), 10
gamblers, 19, 69
Gardner, Archibald, 27, 86, 95, 96, 106, 109, 113, 114, 120, 128
gentiles, 75, 92, 96, 105, 128, 129, 135
Gerrish, Mr., 63, 88
Gilbert and Gerrish, 88
Gillespie, Franklin David, 132, 134
Gillespie, Robert Hemphill, 132, 133, 134
Gillespie, Robert, Jr., 133
Gillilam, John, 10
Gilson, H., 124
Golden, Bob, 100
Gove, Jesse A., 75
Gove, Maria, 75
grand jury, 79, 107, 112, 125, 126
Grant, George D., 29, 31, 70, 79, 91, 127
Grant, Jedediah, 42
grasshoppers, 61
Green River County, 71, 73, 74, 77
Green River Ferry Co., 45
Grimmits, 132
grist mill, 109
Groesbeck, Mr., 63
guns, 8, 9, 18, 33, 69, 76, 77, 89, 97, 105, 124
Gurson, Lewis C., 105

H

Half-Breed Tract, 10
Hammond, William W., 75
Ham's Fork, 45, 74, 75
Hancock County (IL), 14
Hanks, Ephraim, 12, 20, 40, 60, 64, 79, 99
Harding, Stephen S., 104, 105
Harker, Joseph, 30
Harrison, Charles, 87, 97
Hart, Garland, 60
Hartley, Jesse T., 43, 44
Harvey, John, 79
Hatch, Ike, 32
Hatch, Ira, 13
Hawley, William, 45
Hawkes, B., 48
Hawley, Thompson & McDonald Co., 42
Heath, George, 87, 112
Henderson, John, 10
Henderson, Samuel, 10
Henefer, William, 62
Hetherinton, Mary Jane. *See* Hickman, Mary Jane Hetherington
Heywood, Elder, 95
Heywood, Joseph L., 43, 48
Hickman, Avis, 2
Hickman, Bernetta Burckhardt, 5, 6, 7, 9, 14, 15, 22, 27, 39, 45, 52, 54, 93, 97, 119, 130, 131, 132, 133, 134, 135
Hickman, Bill, Jr., 117
Hickman, Diana Case, 54, 62
Hickman, Edwin Temple, 2, 3, 4, 7, 20
Hickman, Edwin Thomas, 9
Hickman, Elizabeth, 9
Hickman, Elizabeth Adams, 3, 4
Hickman Fort, 28
Hickman, George, 124, 135
Hickman, George Washington, 20, 36, 37, 43, 44, 53, 64, 75, 76, 77, 87, 90, 96, 132
Hickman, Hannah Diantha Horr, 41, 62, 98, 113
Hickman Hounds. *See* Hickman, William Adams
Hickman, James Barton, 3, 87, 99
Hickman, Joshua, 9
Hickman, Josiah, 9
Hickman, Katharine, 15, 127, 139
Hickman, Laura Isbella, 71, 123
Hickman, Lettice, 4
Hickman, Luke Johnson, 65
Hickman, Martin, 88
Hickman, Margaret, 52, 56
Hickman, Margaret Rose, 65
Hickman, Mary, 98
Hickman, Mary Ella, 117
Hickman, Mary Jane Hetherington, 85, 116,

119, 120
Hickman, Mary Lucretia Horr, 62, 113
Hickman, Minerva, 13, 16, 21, 22, 27, 30, 54, 65, 93, 116, 117, 118, 119
Hickman, Minerva Lerona, 97, 98, 99, 114, 115
Hickman, Nathaniel, 2
Hickman, Phoebe Delilah, 2, 132, 133
Hickman, Rebecca, 9
Hickman, Rhoda, 4, 132
Hickman, Samuel, 86
Hickman, Sarah Basford Meacham, 30, 54, 119, 132
Hickman, Sarah Katherine, 9, 113, 118, 119
Hickman, Sarah Elizabeth Virginia Johnson, 52, 65, 71, 123, 124
Hickman, Thomas Jefferson, 37, 64, 75, 76, 78, 87, 88
Hickman, Warren E., 87
Hickman, Grandfather William, 2, 4
Hickman, William Adams: bodyguard, 9, 12, 15, 20, 24; *Brigham's Destroying Angel*, x-xi, 127, 129; borrowed money, 97; bought stolen goods, 112; burial, 134; church callings, ordinations, 6-7, 7-8, 9, 12, 13, 14, 15, 16, 20, 24, 29, 31, 32, 39, 43, 48, 62, 71, 80, 85, 119, 120; court actions, 10, 11, 54, 57, 79, 85, 86, 95-101, 106, 108, 111, 112, 117, 123-28; crippled, 93, 124; crossing plains, 24, 25; Danites, Hickman Hounds, 11, 12, 13, 14, 15, 18, 31, 40, 76, 84, 87, 93, 100, 101, 103, 108, 125, 126, 127; death, 129, 133, 134; disfellowshipped, 24, 95; endowed, 14; excommunication, 119, 120; Fairfield (UT), 53, 70, 90, 104, 119, 121, 123, 130, 131; family, 1, 2, 3, 4, 5, 13, 14, 54, 55, 62, 64, 85, 92, 93, 98, 99, 103, 112, 113, 114, 116, 117, 123, 124; farmer, 112; first fight, 7; food for Mormon immigrants, 7; Fort Bridger, 32, 35, 36, 37, 39, 40, 41, 42, 45, 45, 48, 51, 52, 53, 54, 55, 56, 57, 60, 61, 131; gentile, regarded as, 121; government employee, guide, 105, 109-14, 116; Green River County, 31, 33, 35, 36, 37, 38, 41, 42, 43, 44, 45, 46, 47, 48, 49, 51, 52, 53, 54, 55, 63, 65, 66, 117, 131; Illinois, 9, 10, 11, 12, 13, 18; Indians, 6, 12, 19, 20, 23, 24, 28, 29, 30, 35, 37, 39, 45, 46, 47, 48, 56, 60, 99, 109, 110, 111, 114, 116, 117; Lander (WY), 1, 129-35; law, study of, 4, 37, 38, 43, 44, 45, 52, 53, 107, 110, 123; lawmen, 12, 32; mail and express, 20,
59, 60, 61, 62, 63, 64, 65, 66; marriage, 5, 6; marshall, 43; military service, 112; mining, 20, 30, 31, 36, 51, 99, 103, 108, 109, 110, 116, 120; Missouri, 4, 6, 7, 8, 9; Mormon War, 13, 40, 59, 60, 65, 67-81, 84; "The Notorious," 124, 126, 129, 130, 134, 135; pardoned, 80, 113; paranoid, 108; physical appearance, 8; polygamy, 5, 13, 14, 15, 16, 21, 22, 62, 98, 113, 115, 117, 119, 125, 128; poor assisted by, 16; posse, 111; prayers, 92, 97; prison, 127, 129, 130; profanity, 92; protective custody, 129; rebaptism, 120; sheriff, 43; sinister, 110; stealing from gentiles, 96, 106, 108, 111, 112; stood up to Brigham Young, 110; tax collector, 43; Taylorsville (UT), 27, 28, 36, 54, 55, 65, 74, 79, 88, 100, 105, 106, 117; territorial representative, 43; tithing, 113; typhoid fever, 130; Winter Quarters, 12, 14, 16, 19, 20, 21, 22, 23, 24, 25
Hobbs, Dr., 93
Hockaday, John, 60
Hoffman, William, 83
Holeman, J. H., 37, 38
Hopper, William H., 71
Horr, Hannah Diantha. *See* Hickman, Hannah Dinatha Horr
Horr, Mary Lucretia. *See* Hickman, Mary Lucretia Horr
Hudson, Mr., 132
Hunter, Edward, 31, 96
Huntington, Dimick B., 39, 48
Huntington, Lott, 39, 87, 88, 89, 90, 91, 100, 101
Huntsville (IA), 5, 7, 11
Hyde, Orson, 19, 20, 23, 24, 28, 42, 43, 44, 76, 96

I

Idaho, 71
Illinois, 14, 104
Independence (MO), 61, 63
Independence Rock, 60
Indian agents, 23, 99, 110
invasion (U.S. Army), 68, 69, 70, 71
Iowa, 10-11, 85
Irish Ned, 103
ironworks, 73
Irving, John, 100
Isbell family, 2, 3

J

Jackson County (MO), 6

jail, 10, 18
Jensen, John, 105
Joe, 32
Joe (Spaniard), 48
Johnson, Dunkin, 21
Johnson, Joachim, 84, 86, 88, 90, 93, 100
Johnson, Luke, 52, 53, 123
Johnson, Sarah Elizabeth. *See* Hickman, Sarah Elizabeth Johnson
Johnson, S. M., 97
Johnston, Albert Sidney, 6, 40, 67, 68, 74, 75, 76, 78, 83, 85, 90, 104
Jones, Andrew J., 69, 70
Jones, Benjamin, 25
Jones, "Buck," 70
Jones, Daniel, 63, 78, 79
Jones, Emory, 10
Jones, J. H., 45
Jones, N. V., 77
Jones, William, 105
Jordan River (UT), 27, 28, 80, 104
Jordan Silver Mining Co., 110
Jordan Ward (LDS), 24
Josephites, 115
Juab County (UT), 53

K

Kanesville (IA). *See* Winter Quarters
Kane, Thomas L., 16, 80
Kansas, 87, 88, 129
Kearney (NE), 60
Kell, Timothy, 11
Kentucky, 1, 2, 4
Keokuk (IA), 10, 126
Kerr, John, 45
Kimball, Heber C., 13, 14, 20, 31, 79, 80, 96
Kimball, Hiram, 61
Kimball, William, 31, 39, 41, 70, 77, 78, 127
Kinny's Point (WY), 44

L

Lander Hotel, 133, 134
Laramie (WY), 116
larceny, 11
Laub, George, 89
Laurence, J. W., 116, 117
Lea, L., 37, 38
Leanderback, Daniel, 11
Lee County (IA), 10, 18, 19
Lee, John D., 24, 128
Lehi (UT), 130
Leonard, Bradford, 97
Lewis, Martha, 21

Lewis, Tarlton, 11
Lincoln, Abraham, 104
Lisonbee, Eda Kohlhepp, 28
Little Cottonwood Canyon, 112
Little, Feramorz, 60, 61
Little, J. D., 41
Little, Jesse C., 48, 53
Little Mountain (UT), 99
Little Soldier, 110, 111
Livingston & Kinkaid, 73
Los Angeles (CA), 69
Lott, John, 70
Lott, Peter, 11
Luce, Jason, 87, 90, 91, 93, 100, 107, 108
Luce, John Martin, 87, 100, 108
Luce, Sarah, 14, 15, 20
Luce, Wilford, 87, 100, 101, 108
Lyman, Amasa, 20, 89

M

Macon County (MO), 6
mail, 110, 111
Marcy, R. B., 40
Marcy, William, 59
Margaret. *See* Hickman, Margaret
Markham, Brother, 65, 66
Marshall, P. E., 36
martial law, 69
Martineau, James Henry, 68
Mason, Charles, 10
Massacre, Mountain Meadows, 69, 128
Matthews, Presley, 11
McKean, James, 124, 126, 128
McNeal, Franklin, 69
Macky, J., 56
McCann, J. P., 11
McGraw-Hockaday Line, 60, 66
McGraw, W. M. F., 56, 60, 61, 63
Meacham, Emory, 87
Meacham, Jeremiah, 28
Meacham, Morris, 127
Meacham, Samuel, 78, 87
Merrill, D. C., 36
Methodist church, 6, 7
Mexico, 16, 38
Miles, Stephen B., 64
Militia, Mormon, 28, 38, 68, 69, 72, 73, 74, 126
Miller's Hollow (IA), 22
Minute Men, 31
Mississippi River, 10, 14, 16
Missouri, 114, 115, 118
Missouri River, 3, 19, 64, 73
mob(s), 73

Monaghan, Tom, 129
Mona Lakes (UT), 70
Montana, 100, 103, 105
Montrose (IA), 10, 21
"Monty" Jack, 62
Moore, David, 48
Mormon Battalion, 16, 21
Mormon Ferry, 45
Mormon Gulch, 116
Moreno, Frank, 123
Morrisite Affair, 103-108, 127
Morris, Joseph, 104, 105
Morton, Doc, 37
Mosquito Creek (IA), 22
Mount Pisgah (IA), 21
mountain men, 36, 38, 40, 41, 42, 44, 45, 46, 47, 53, 71, 73, 75, 85
mules, 111
Mumford, "Brother," 63
Murdock, John, 70

N

Nash, Marie Kohlhepp, 54
Nashville (IA), 10
Nauvoo (IL), 9, 10, 11, 12, 13, 14, 15, 16, 17, 19, 21
Nauvoo War, 12, 18
Nebeker, John, 42
Nebraska, 85
Neibaur, Isaac, 87, 100
Nelson, John, 112
Nephi (UT), 70, 71, 131, 135
Nevada, 105
New Jerusalem (MO), 6
New York, 118, 126, 130
Nicoles, Alvin, 7
North Platte River, 60

O

oath, 15
Ogden (UT), 35, 48, 51, 86, 131, 135
Ohio, 6
Omaha Indians, 23, 24
Oregon, 37, 43, 44, 98, 107
Orem (UT), 83
Oquirrh Mountains, 123, 124

P

Pacific Springs (WY), 36, 44
Parowan (UT), 72
Parley's Canyon (UT), 131
Pawnee Indians, 23, 24

peace treaty, 111
Perry, M., 76, 77
persecution, 72
Peterson, Mr., 132
Phelps, William, 31
Pioneer Fort, 27
Placerville (CA), 30, 119
Platte Bridge, 63
Pleasanton, Captain, 71
Pocatello (ID), 117
Point of the Mountain (UT), 110
Pond Town (UT), 80
Popo Agie Valley (WY), 134
Pottowattomie County (IA), 19, 20
Pratt, Orson, 31, 61
Pratt, Parley P., 14
Provo Indian War, 28, 29, 110, 111
Provo (UT), 28, 29, 43, 44, 71, 110

Q

Quincy (IL), 11

R

Randolph County (MO), 4, 5, 6, 64
Ransohff, N. S., 112
rebellion, 79
Redwood Road, 80
Reeside, John E., 60
Reformation, Mormon, 61, 71
refugees, 80
Reorganized Church of Jesus Christ of Latter Day Saints, 115
Reynolds, Wood, 87, 100
Rhodes, James, 87, 112
Rhodes, Joe, 69, 93, 108
Rich, Charles C., 31
Rich, O. H., 11
Richards, Willard, 31
Ripley, Doc, 30
Robinson, Jack, 45, 46, 47
Robinson, J. King, 117
Robison, Lewis, 32, 38, 40, 41, 42, 48, 49, 51, 52, 56, 79
Rock Canyon (UT), 29
Rockwell, Orrin Porter, 9, 12, 31, 32, 40, 47, 55, 61, 62, 70, 71, 79, 85, 88, 90, 91, 100, 116, 127
Rogers, Mr., 132
Ruby Valley, 99
Rush Valley (UT), 28, 29, 53, 71, 80, 83, 100, 111, 121, 124
Russell, Fell, 45
Russell, John, 44, 45

Russell, Majors & Waddell, 75
Ryan, Elisha, 40, 41, 42, 44, 46, 47, 48
Ryan, Tom, 116

S

Sac Indians, 6
St. Clair, 84
St. George (UT), 127, 128
St. Joseph (MO), 64
St. Louis (MO), 14, 137
Salem (UT), 80
Salsbury, Wilkins G., 11
Salt River (MO), 7
San Bernardino (CA), 70
San Francisco (CA), 118
San Pete Valley (UT), 85
Santa Fe (NM), 69
schools, 2, 3, 5, 6, 98, 113
Scott, Camp, 79
Scott, John, 15
Selden, H. R., 85
Shambip County (UT), 53
Shaver, Leonidas, 39, 48
Sherman, Edwin, 124
Shipps, Richard W., 9
Shoshones, 39, 40, 46, 47, 52, 56
silver mining, 109, 110
Sioux, 116
slave owners, 3
Smith, Alexander, 115, 118
Smith, C. F., 74
Smith, Colonel, 74
Smith, David, 115, 118
Smith, Elias, 32, 42, 57, 97, 100
Smith, Emma, 13
Smith, Ettie V., 44
Smith, George A., 31, 36, 68, 72, 86
Smith, Hyrum, 11, 13, 14
Smith, John P., 87, 100, 101, 133
Smith, "Uncle" John, 115
Smith, Joseph, 9, 11, 12, 13, 14
Smith, Joseph III, 115, 118
Smith, Lot, 9, 55, 71, 73, 79
Smith, Major, 69
Smith, William, 12
Snake (Indians), 57
Snake River (ID), 47
Snow, Eliza R., 13
Social Hall, 71
Soda Springs (ID), 105, 111
South Pass (WY), 25, 51, 56, 75, 116
Spanish Fork (UT), 28, 80, 110
Spanish Frank, 123, 124
Spencer, Claudius V., 53

spies, 12, 15, 75, 77, 114
squatters, 3
Stenhouse, T. B. H., 85
Stevens, Charles, 25
Stockton (UT), 120
Stoddard, Rufus, 40
Stokes County (NC), 2, 3
Stout, Hosea, 9, 11, 42, 43, 45, 48, 54, 56, 70, 77, 78, 84, 127
Stowell, William, 79
Stringham, Bryant, 121
Surry County (NC), 2, 3
Swazey, Rodney D., 86
Sweetwater River (WY), 24, 38, 51, 60, 65, 66, 74, 116
Swift River (IA), 21

T

temple(s), 14, 61, 115
Tanner, Brother, 30
Taylor, John, 28, 79
Taylor, Joseph, 73, 79
Taylor, Zachary, 43, 56, 60
teamsters, 74, 75
telegraph, 110
Terry, Joshua, 62, 79
thieves, 83, 89, 95
tobacco, 2
Tooele County (UT), 53, 121, 123, 126
Townsend Hotel, 89, 91
Tracy, Albert, 77
Traskolowshi, Joseph, 57
treason, 79, 80
Tullidge, Edward, 28, 29
Tuttle, Newton, 73
Twitchell, Mr., 48

U

Union Pacific Railroad, 133
Union Vedette, 109
United Order, 104
"Use Him Up, Bill," 129
Utah Lake, 28, 80, 111
Utes, 29, 37, 48, 110, 111

V

Valley Tan, 80, 84
Van Vliet, Stewart, 71, 72, 75
Vasquez, Louis, 32, 38, 40, 41, 48, 52
Vaughn, Mr., 33
Virginia City (NV), 119

W

Wade, Edward, 21, 117
Wade, Minverva. *See* Hickman, Minerva
Wade, Moses, 16, 21, 22
Wade, Sally Maria Bundy, 21, 22 Waite, Colonel, 76
Wakara, 35, 37
Wakeley, John, 87, 90, 91, 97
Walker, Charles, 93
Walker, Lucy, 13, 14
Walker War, 35
Walker, William H., 11, 40
Warm Springs, 70
Warren County (KY), 2, 3
Washakie, 56
Washington, D.C., 20, 46, 53, 56, 57, 64, 67, 74, 114
Weber (UT), 38, 70, 71, 105
Wells, Daniel H., 18, 28, 29, 31, 39, 69, 73, 77, 79, 80, 86, 127
West Canyon (UT), 130
West Jordan Mining District, 110
West Jordan Ward (LDS), 80, 85, 92, 95
Wheeler, Dick, 87, 91
Wheeler, Thomas J., 87, 88
Whigs, 19
whiskey, 78, 92, 106, 113
Whitney, Orson F., 105
Willard, Nathan, 130
Williams, Colonel, 13
Willie & Martin Handcart Co., 54
Wind River Mountains, 48, 51, 132
Winter Quarters, 19
Woodard, Charles, 62
Woodard, Heber, 62
Woodland, Bill, 87, 90
Woodly, John, 100
Wood, Malinda, 14
Woodrings, 132
Woodruff, Wilford, 31, 53, 76, 107, 108
Woodson, Samuel H., 60
Woolley, Edward D., 31
Work, William, 3
Wright, Furguson, 10
Wright, John, 10
Wright, "Tuck," 69, 70
Wyoming, 108, 116, 129, 131, 132

Y

Yates, Richard, 77, 78, 125
Young, Brigham H., 16, 18
Young, Brigham, Jr., 19
Young, Brigham, 12, 13, 15, 16, 19, 20, 22, 24, 28, 31, 32, 33, 36, 37, 39, 40, 42, 43, 45, 47, 48, 52, 53, 56, 59, 60, 61, 64, 65, 67, 68, 69, 70, 71, 72, 73, 75, 77, 78, 79, 80, 83, 84, 85, 86, 87, 89, 90, 92, 97, 98, 99, 104, 105, 106, 108, 109, 110, 112, 115, 116, 118, 119, 120, 121, 124, 125, 126, 127, 128, 131
Young, John, 62, 77
Young, Joseph A., 31, 77, 127
Young, Phineas, 16, 18, 79
Young, William, 79